Spinning the Web

Spinning the Web

A Handbook for Public Relations on the Internet

Diane F. Witmer
California State University, Fullerton

 LONGMAN

An imprint of Addison Wesley Longman, Inc.

New York • Reading, Massachusetts • Menlo Park, California • Harlow, England
Don Mills, Ontario • Sydney • Mexico City • Madrid • Amsterdam

Editor in Chief: Priscilla McGeehon
Acquisitions Editor: Michael Greer
Marketing Manager: Megan Galvin-Fak
Cover Designer: John Callahan
Cover Illustration: PhotoDisc
Senior Print Buyer: Hugh Crawford
Printer and Binder: Maple Press
Cover Printer: Coral Graphics

Please visit our website at http://www.awlonline.com

ISBN 0-321-07713-X

1 2 3 4 5 6 7 8 9 10 — MA — 02 01 00 99

Snelot

Contents

Chapter 3. Overview of Computer-Mediated Communication 51

Chapter 4. Research 81

Chapter 5. Planning 109

Chapter 6. Execution 125

Contents

Introduction & Overview

If you were asked to develop a Web presence for your
client, where would you start? If you needed to find
out how many American homes had VCRs, where
would you look? If you wanted to observe candid
conversations between your client's consumers,
where would you go? This handbook answers those
questions, as well as others that arise when practicing
public relations, and offers solutions that utilize the
Internet.

This book focuses on the connections between public
relations and communication technology. That means
it necessarily includes an introduction to that
technology. However, it is not a technical book, nor it
is it targeted to technicians. Rather, it is a handbook
for Internet *users* who work in the field of public
relations. This means that although the text does
review basic processes in order to contextualize
public relations for practice in the electronic
environment, it targets the reader who has some
understanding of basic public relations goals,
strategies, tools, and functions. The aim is twofold:

1. to help you, as a practicing or future public
    relations professional, understand both the
    capabilities and the limitations of Internet
    technology for attaining PR goals and objectives,
    and
2. to guide you in developing basic Internet literacy,
    including a general understanding of how to

develop and construct simple Web pages, in order to communicate intelligently with Web designers and other technical people with whom you might work.

Because Internet-based resources tend to change before a book sees print, this text does not include extensive listings of Web sites. However, up-to-date pointers and links to a variety of resources can be found in the online supplement to this text. Topics for which additional materials may be found on the Web are marked with a "Check the Web" icon in the left margin like the one on this page.

Computer-mediated communication encompasses interpersonal, group, organizational, and public communications. It therefore challenges us to think in new ways that encompass a broad range of traditional communication models and theories. As a result, this handbook does not segment the field of communication into subspecialties. Instead, it draws from a variety of fields across the discipline to depict generic models of communication and to develop a theoretical framework for understanding public relations on the Internet.

The body of this book is organized, in part, according to the four-step public relations process, after first laying the technological and theoretical groundwork for understanding the public relations process and its relationship to the Internet. The text begins with an overview of computers and computer networking, and then provides a foundation for understanding both the nature and processes of public relations and of computer-mediated communication. It then describes the role the Internet might play in each step of the four-step public relations process. The book also explores some special applications of the Internet for public relations, and outlines some specific cases where the Internet was an important aspect of a communication campaign or program. Finally, this text addresses some of the ethical and legal issues we face in cyberspace.

The first chapter describes the differences between the ways we use computers and various types of software, and provides a basis for understanding the terminology of the Internet. The second and third chapters offer theoretical models and perspectives that help our understanding of the communication process and its relationship to technology, with special emphasis on public relations as a form of communication.

The fourth, fifth, sixth, and seventh chapters each address one step of the four-step public relations process: research, planning, execution, and evaluation. The approach in all of these four chapters is two-pronged. First, each chapter briefly describes ways in which the Internet can be used within the context of the four-step process for developing any campaign or program. Then, each chapter focuses on specific aspects of the particular step it addresses for the specific purpose of Web site development. As a result, you can use this handbook both as a "starter kit" for developing Internet-based strategies and as a reference for enhancing your campaign and program development with Internet-based tools.

The eighth chapter describes some of the ways in which the Internet is enhancing consumer relations, investor relations, crisis communications, and more.

It also explores the rapidly growing field of electronic commerce, which presents enormous new opportunities and challenges for public relations practitioners. Finally, the ninth chapter addresses the ethical and legal implications of electronic public relations, including eye-opening tips on recognizing and combating Internet hoaxes and urban legends.

Given the negative connotations that "spin" has for the field of public relations, you might wonder why I would use such a word in the title of this text. The answer, of course, is partly because of the play on words. In keeping with the World Wide Web metaphor, we might be said to be spinning our Web sites as we spin our messages. Perhaps more important, I've adopted a popular and long-standing linguistic strategy of appropriating a negative term for positive use. In this case, I'm using the term "spin" to indicate a sense of advocacy, persuasion, and perspective—but not to imply in any way unethical or manipulative persuasion tactics. On the contrary, this book emphasizes the ethical challenges we face when we use the Internet, and encourages practitioners to adhere to the highest ethical and moral standards in all their endeavors.

Some public relations educators and researchers propose that truly excellent and ethical public relations practices do not advocate, but rather play a role of mediation between a client and its publics. While this idea has merit, there are other ways to approach public relations and its messages. One way is from a rhetorical perspective.

As far back as Aristotle, rhetoric has been recognized as a persuasive art of speaking well. That means a view of public relations in the rhetorical tradition and as a rhetorical endeavor characterizes all public relations work as inherently persuasive. Therefore, public relations practitioners cannot help but assume some level of advocacy for the client. We persuade our clients to consider emergent issues; we persuade target publics to purchase our clients' products; we persuade employees that their service to the company is appreciated; and we persuade editors that our stories are newsworthy. In other words, we do, indeed, "spin," and the pioneers of our field, including Edward Bernays and Ivy Ledbetter Lee, acknowledged that fact as they systematically engaged in persuasive communications.

But persuasion is not synonymous with manipulation, and spinning does not mean we can or should hide the truth, write unbalanced stories, use inappropriate propaganda techniques, or omit important facts. Rather, it underscores our responsibility to be fully disclosive, to strengthen our arguments with opposing points of view and counter-arguments, and to be forthcoming with all the information we have at our disposal. Thus, in a metaphorical sense, we might think of our spinning, both on the Web and off, as that of a top, whirling in the direction of our goals and objectives—and always balanced on point.

This book, like any writing project, is a collaborative endeavor in which countless people have been involved and to whom I am indebted. I especially thank the many students who have asked probing questions, made suggestions, brought me articles and Web site URLs, and perhaps most important, prodded me to learn and share whatever I could absorb about emergent computer technologies. I also thank Coral

Ohl for helping me work out knotty phrasing, and the anonymous Longman reviewers for their very helpful suggestions. Finally, I thank my family for its longsuffering patience during the incalculable hours that I was lost in cyberspace, with a special thanks to my mother for keeping the laundry going while I stared into a computer monitor.

Diane F. Witmer
Fullerton, CA

Chapter 1. Overview of Communication Technologies

Understanding & Using Computers & Computer Networks

Learning Objectives

In this chapter, you will learn about your relationships with computer networks and the software that makes computers "smart." Topics covered in this chapter include:

➤ System and application software.
➤ Four levels of computer networking.
➤ Communication software for different types of computer networking.
➤ What all those letters mean in Web and e-mail "addresses."

Communicating through Computers

Human efforts to communicate across space and time can be traced to prehistoric cave paintings where artwork on the walls represented hunting expeditions. But the nature of the cave drawings cannot fully communicate the experience of the hunt. Pigment colors, cave surfaces, and artists' skills affect the ways in which the experience is expressed. Thus, the medium through which communication occurs alters the expression of an experience. Today, of course, much of our communication is conducted through keystrokes rather than through brush strokes.

Communication is mediated whenever something other than the sender and receiver is involved in the transmission or receipt of the message. Because the types of computer technologies we use mediate the nature of our communications, scholars have coined the term computer-mediated communication (CMC) to encompass a broad variety of online communicative processes. Whether we're engaged in one-on-one (interpersonal) conversations, group work, advertising, public relations, marketing, consumerism, or democratic processes, if we're using computers, we can classify our activities as forms of CMC.

Computers are everywhere. They are both ubiquitous and pervasive in contemporary living. We use them every day to communicate, often without thinking about it. When we slide a bank debit card in an automated teller machine (ATM), use a touch-screen bridal registry, leave a voice mail message, or scan a discount card at the grocery store, we're really communicating with and through a computer. But as anyone who as tried to learn a new computer system knows, using computers isn't always as simple as swiping a card or touching a monitor screen.

Just logging onto an e-mail account for the first time can be a daunting experience. For starters, computer terminology sometimes has multiple meanings. "Kermit," for example, is the name of both a program application and a protocol for transferring data between computers. Worse yet, both the language of computers and the naming of the software create metaphoric and semantic chaos.

Computers are metaphorical tools, servants, work areas, filing systems, and spatial areas. We fill them as containers of digitized data, travel through time and space along virtual highways, and work and play in cybercommunities. Our immediate interaction is with keyboard, screen, and central processing unit (CPU), but our most vital activities may be accomplished with software applications that are housed on a distant computer.

We speak of signing in or logging on, but to what? When we send e-mail, where does it go? And where is it when the recipient logs onto an account at a distant computer to read it? This chapter answers those questions. As a result, it is the most "technical" portion of the book.

You may question the need to understand any of the technical aspects of CMC. After all, you don't need to memorize all the components of an internal combustion engine in order to drive a car. But the more you know about your vehicle, the better equipped you are to maintain it, respond to on-the-road emergencies like flat tires and smoking engines, or communicate with mechanics when your car needs maintenance or repair. The same concept holds true for the practice of public relations on the Internet. If you know something about how computers communicate and how Web pages are put together, you're in a good position to communicate intelligently with Web designers, computer system administrators, and clients.

In the next few pages, we'll focus on personal computers, since they are the most widely used communications tools, and explore the general nature of computer systems and software. One topic the next few sections of this chapter will address is what software applications do, and how applications for communicating through the Internet differ from non-communication applications.

System & Application Software

One of the first points of confusion in CMC occurs the moment the computer power is switched on. Computers really can't do much unless they have the proper software installed that enables them to function. An IBM-compatible or Macintosh-compatible computer is just a hunk of plastic, chips, and wires without software.

Computer Operating Systems

The most basic level of software is the operating
system or OS. Usually, when you turn on your
computer, the OS is automatically launched. The OS
tells your computer whether it's a Mac or an IBM,
and manages all the computer's files and software
applications. It also keeps track of the random access
memory or RAM your computer has and how much is
being used for each application. RAM is computer
memory that can be accessed randomly, and it is
erased whenever the power is shut off. That is one
reason you might lose unsaved work if a power glitch
shuts down your computer in the middle of a task.
Your whole document is held only in RAM until it is
saved to a hard disk, floppy diskette, Zip disk, or
some other medium.

Beyond managing files and applications, the OS
controls input of data from the keyboard, mouse, or
touch screen, and output to printer, monitor, and other
peripheral devices. Examples of widely used
operating systems for personal computers include
DOS, Windows, Windows NT, and Macintosh OS.
Sun Microsystems computers use an OS called Unix.
If you use the Internet, you've probably already
communicated with a computer that has a Unix OS.

Once your computer is up and running, the OS
typically will allow you to perform some simple
tasks, such as viewing the date and time. It also
displays directories of files, and shows the files and
applications within those directories. Both Windows
and the Mac OS display directories as "file folder"
icons. The files within the folders are represented as
application-specific icons. For example, a letter

written with Microsoft Word looks like a tiny
document with a "W" on it to indicate it is a Word
file.

Computer Applications

Application software (sometimes called applications
or programs) is the term for any specialized software
that is designed to accomplish specific tasks on a
computer. Microsoft Word is an example of an
application that is used for word processing and
desktop publishing. Different versions are produced
for different operating systems, and many software
developers use keyboard commands that are standard
for specific systems. For example, "control+o" is the
standard Windows keyboard command to open a file,
and "command+o" (sometimes called "Apple key
+o") is the equivalent command for the Mac OS. In
both the Windows and the Mac environments,
software applications typically open only documents
that were created in those applications, unless the
applications have built-in translators. For example,
Microsoft Word can open documents that were
created in Word, and it also can translate documents
that were created in some versions of WordPerfect,
Microsoft Works, and a variety of Web page editors.

Although the basic concepts of operating systems and
applications may seem simple, they can become
pretty confusing when you're connected to other
computers. Therefore, in order to use the Web and
Internet effectively for public relations, it's helpful to
develop some understanding of different types of
computer networks and the software used for each.

Levels of Computer Networking

It's easiest to think of computer networks in terms of four levels of use:

1. Stand-alone computer.
2. Local Area Network (LAN).
3. Wide Area Network (WAN).
4. Internet and World Wide Web (WWW).

Different types of networks can require different types of software. But how do you know which is which? Well, although the categories aren't mutually exclusive, you can get a rough idea of which type of network you're using based on the physical space it covers. When you use an ATM, you're probably using a WAN because you are communicating with a mainframe computer that is some distance away; when you use a networked computer lab, you're probably using a LAN because the lab computers are connected within one building or cluster of buildings. Each type of network often has other characteristics that enable you to perform different types of tasks.

Stand-Alone Computers

Although a computer may be connected to a network, it often isn't used for direct communication. Most business professionals use stand-alone computers for a variety of tasks, including word processing, spreadsheet analysis, desktop publishing, bookkeeping, and graphic design. Stand-alone use can be characterized by the following characteristics:

> ➤ The tasks do not require that the computer communicate with anything other than a local peripheral device such as a printer or scanner.
> ➤ The tasks involve only creating or modifying files and saving them to a hard disk or diskette.
> ➤ The computer uses its OS and retains its native attributes. For example, if you're using an IBM-compatible computer or an Apple Macintosh, the OS and applications will look and behave like typical Windows, DOS, or Mac software.

Examples of tasks you might accomplish using a stand-alone computer include:

> ➤ Creating a report in Microsoft Word or WordPerfect and saving it to a diskette.
> ➤ Record keeping using Microsoft Excel.
> ➤ Designing a tri-fold brochure using Adobe PageMaker.
> ➤ Printing a document on a printer that is dedicated to the stand-alone computer.

Local Area Networks (LANs)

LANs typically cover a small physical area, such as a room or a building or a group of buildings. In a LAN, several computers are connected by cable, and the computers generally are similar. Thus, the computers usually are all IBM compatible or all Apple Macintosh compatible.

One common use of a LAN is the computer lab, in which a number of computers are connected to each other and to a server. The server is a computer that is specifically designated to provide access to shared files and software applications for all authorized computers on the network. You may use shared software applications on a LAN to perform stand-alone type tasks, such as word processing, desktop publishing, or spread sheets, but you also can accomplish tasks that require sharing or exchanging files. LANs often can be identified by the following key characteristics:

Similar work stations or personal computers are connected by cable or Ethernet over a small physical area. Ethernet is a specialized combination of software and hardware that enables transfer of data between computers. Because each computer on the network has its own central processing unit (CPU), the computers can execute commands and use their native operating systems and attributes. This means Apple computers behave like Apples, and IBM-compatibles behave like IBM computers. As a result, when you share files through a LAN, you often can move the files between your computer and other computers just as if you were moving them around on your own computer. Special networking software allows the computers to communicate through the network. Usually, no special knowledge of the networking software is required of the individual users whose computers are connected to the network.

Stand-alone type tasks can be accomplished on a LAN, but may require software applications or files that are accessed from a central server. For example, if you're writing a memo on a computer that's part of a LAN, your word processing program may not be installed on the computer at your desk, but may be "served" to your computer from a specially designated computer.

Examples of common uses for locally networked
computers include:

➢ Sharing files to edit the copy of a newsletter.
➢ Printing a document on a printer that is shared
  among several or all of the computers on the
  network.
➢ Accessing Microsoft PowerPoint from a
  designated server to develop a slide presentation.
  When you're using a networked version of an
  application, it may appear to reside on your local
  computer, but it will not run unless the server is
  running.
➢ Shared scheduling and project management.
➢ Group decision support systems (GDSSs), which
  enable users to anonymously express opinions and
  vote on issues.

Wide Area Networks (WANs)

As the name implies, WANs generally cover large
physical areas, and can span huge areas. They
typically are more sophisticated than LANs, and may
include one or many types of computers, including
mainframe computers. A WAN often consists of
multiple LANs, and the computers may be connected
through public utilities, such as a telephone company
or television cable provider.

Large corporations often use WANs to communicate
across wide geographical areas for file sharing,
collaboration across distances, project management,
and electronic commerce. WANs often can be
identified by the following key characteristics:

> The connected computers may be of different brands and capacities.
> The network covers a large physical area.
> The computers on the network may or may not have their own CPUs. They sometimes are designated to accomplish only limited types of tasks, such as a credit card approval system, or they may be capable of executing sophisticated and complex tasks.
> The computers require a special networking language or protocol to allow communication and file sharing between different operating systems.
> A special OS may be used at a host computer for multi-user functions such as file storage and e-mail. One OS that is widely used for such purposes is Unix. Originally developed by Bell Labs, Unix is designed for multiple users. Although Unix is not user friendly, it is a powerful OS that can be accessed from remote computers, and it allows users to perform a variety of online tasks.

Examples of common uses for wide area networks include:

> Making a credit card purchase.
> Ordering a gift through a store's touch-screen registry.
> Using a touch-screen mall directory kiosk.
> Visiting a bank automated teller machine.
> Using a grocery "club" card for instant discounts on purchases.
> Collaboration across distances through the Internet.

> ➢ Distributing electronic newsletters throughout a
>   multinational organization.

The Internet & World Wide Web (WWW)

The largest WAN in existence is the Internet. When
you hook up a modem to your home computer and
use your telephone line to dial up to an Internet
Service Provider (ISP), you are connecting your
computer to a WAN, which, in turn, is connected to
the Internet. The Internet is an amorphous, global
network of networks, and it includes tens of
thousands of LANs and WANs. Because there is no
central administration or oversight for the Internet, it
has been likened to a "wild frontier."

Although we can probably trace its evolution back to
1836 when Cooke and Wheatstone patented the
telegraph, the Internet was born in 1969 under the
name, ARPANET. The project was originally
commissioned by the Department of Defense for
research on networking computers, and by 1971, was
being used for electronic mail (e-mail). By the mid-
1980s, the Internet was widely used in government
and educational institutions.

In 1989, the World Wide Web emerged as an easy
retrieval system for information. Up to that point,
information was accessed through the Internet via
text-based hierarchical directories (the equivalent of
folders on local computers), which were difficult to
search and navigate. Retrieval of a particular
document often required moving from a parent

directory into a lengthy, sequential series of subdirectories.

The Web is actually a specialized portion of the Internet. It consists of computers that are dedicated in whole or in part to serving "hypertext" documents. Hypertext is a specialized form of database system that enables users to navigate between different types of files (including text, audio, image, and video) in a nonlinear fashion. The term was coined by Theodor Nelson as a way to describe what he called "non–sequential writing."

The Web offers an alternative to the older, text-based, hierarchical directory schemes. Hypertext documents allow readers to move from point to point nonsequentially because the information is stored at networked locations or nodes. As a result, you now can access information with a single point-and-click of your mouse, rather than navigating up and down through lengthy lists of hierarchical directories. Figure 1.1 depicts an example of nonsequential Web retrieval. In this example, three documents about Mozart reside on a computer at University Q. Each of those documents contains several "hyperlinks" to other documents about Mozart, his life, or his works. Each link allows the computer user to access a document stored on the same or a different computer. The computer at University Q in Figure 1.1 may be on the other side of the globe from the computer at University R.

In addition to ease of navigation, the Web supports information in a variety of formats, including graphic images, video, 3D interactive images, and audio. As a result, business and public relations messages may be distributed in multimedia formats, rather than strictly as text.

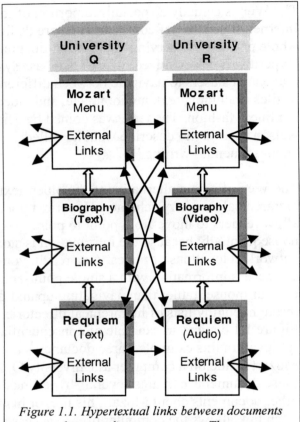

Figure 1.1. Hypertextual links between documents stored on two distant computers. The arrows indicate direct links between the documents shown and to hypertext documents on other computers.

Some of the key characteristics of the Internet and Web include:

➢ Modem, cable modem, or Ethernet connection to an Internet Service Provider (ISP).
➢ Many types of computers and operating systems.

> ➤ Specialized software to access the Internet and Web, to transfer files, to send and receive e-mail, and to view multimedia Web sites.
> ➤ Global coverage by the network.

Examples of ways in which the Web and Internet are used include:

> ➤ Searching for and retrieving U.S. census information through the Web for a research study.
> ➤ Reading national and local newspapers.
> ➤ Listening to radio broadcasts.
> ➤ Computer conferencing.
> ➤ Sending and receiving personal and professional e-mail.
> ➤ Distributing electronic media releases.
> ➤ Providing a 3D visual tour of a resort or hotel.

The Internet and Web have had enormous impact on contemporary business communication and public relations. It is commonplace to see integrated marketing strategies that include commercial advertisements that invite consumers to visit Web sites, and business cards imprinted with e-mail and Web information. Interactive Web-based chats, search engines, bulletin boards, three-dimensional graphics, and video and audio capabilities, coupled with user friendly point-and-click technology, give the Web almost limitless potential for the practice of public relations.

How the World Wide Web Is Spun

In order to use the Web effectively, it's important to have some understanding of how it works. When you access a Web page, you're not really looking at a single "page," even though that's the way it appears on your computer monitor. Web pages are actually text files in which a series of codes, called hypertext markup language (html), tells your Web browser how to display several documents on your screen, including background patterns photos, and other graphic elements, as well as audio or video clips. Every graphic or sound or video element is a different file that may be stored either on the same computer as the basic Web page or on a different computer.

Figure 1.2 depicts the "home" Web page for the Public Relations Society of America (PRSA). Although the page appears as a unified whole on the computer screen, it consists of an html document that includes the text. The html document also tells the Web browser to display that text with nine different graphic elements in a particular arrangement on the screen.

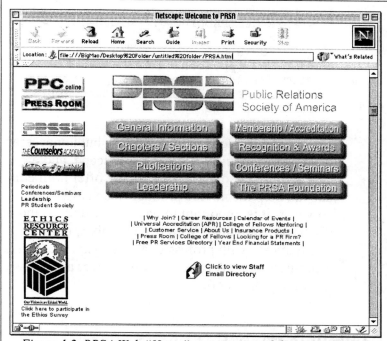

Figure 1.2. PRSA Web "Home" page as viewed through Netscape Navigator. Each graphic image is a separate file. The eight "buttons" in the center constitute one image. Can you spot the eight additional images?

If you were to view the html document for the Web page in Figure 1.2 as text in a word processor, it would look like the fragment of the "home page" code that appears below. This section of the document tells the Web browser, in part, to display the graphic element "`ppcicon.gif`" and to make the graphic a hotlink to a second document that is named "index.html." The "index.html" document resides on the same server as the "home page," but it is in a different directory—the "`ppc`" directory. The directory and file appear names are specified in what we might call html shorthand as "`ppc/index.html`:.

```
<table CELLPADDING="2" width="580">
  <tr>
    <td><a HREF="ppc/index.html">
<img SRC="ppcicon.gif"
WIDTH="114" HEIGHT="32"
    ALT="Professional Practice Center"
BORDER="0"></a>
```

Writing html code is relatively easy, but unnecessary for most of us, since Microsoft, Netscape, and a variety of other software developers offer html editors that can help the novice produce Web pages. However, it is important to have some understanding of what developing a Web page involves in order to communicate with professional Web page designers or programmers. As a result, we'll cover a few basics of html in Chapter 6.

Communication Software

The Internet sometimes intimidates novice users because the software interfaces seem complex and alien. Networking software often isn't as intuitive and friendly as standard personal computer software applications, and it takes some concentration at first to figure out what's going on. Sometimes, it's even difficult to tell what OS you're using.

The first thing you need to access the Internet is communication software that will allow your computer to communicate through the type of connection you have. If you're using a modem, it probably came equipped with the proper software. Your Internet Service Provider (ISP) can help you configure your computer and modem so you can connect to the Internet.

The second thing you need to access the Internet is "client" software, or program applications that will allow you to send e-mail, browse the Web, or read newsgroup postings. In this section, we'll look at the relationships between types of applications, rather than on features of specific applications.

One of the most confusing aspects of using the Internet is the nature of the connections to some host computers. With some program applications, your computer suddenly looks and acts like a different type of computer—usually one that's much less friendly than your comfy Dell or Mac. You often need to use a new set of commands to communicate with the host computer, although you still use your computer's standard commands to launch or quit applications. It's not always easy to remember which computer will accept which command.

Figure 1.3 depicts one example of the ways in which an Internet connection changes the way you use your computer. The small inner "window" is a launched Telnet application with a connection to a remote host computer in place.

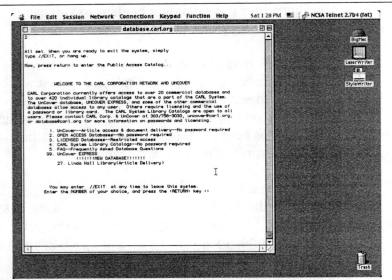

Figure 1.3. Telnet application as it appears on a Macintosh screen. The application is launched using Macintosh commands. All commands executed within the Telnet window affect only transactions on the remote host computer. Commands executed outside the Telnet window affect only transactions on the local personal computer.

Telnet is a protocol that allows computers with different operating systems to communicate over the Internet, and the "client" software for Telnet is available as applications for both IBM-compatible and Macintosh computers. In the case of Figure 1.3, it's being used on a Mac, and the remote "host" computer is running a Unix operating system.

Once a Telnet application is launched and a connection with a host computer is made, all transactions within the Telnet window are done in "terminal emulation." This means that your computer is behaving like or emulating the host computer to which it is connected. Therefore, all commands within the Telnet window affect only the files and directories that are stored on the remote host computer. Moving from the inner window to the desktop moves you from terminal emulation to the Mac (or Windows) OS. Then, commands affect only the files and applications on the local computer. Moving back into the inner window puts you back in terminal emulation and communication with the remote host. The result is that you must use two sets of commands for two different operating systems: 1) your Windows or Mac commands to launch or quit the application, or to close the Telnet window, and 2) the commands for the OS of the remote host computer within the Telnet window.

Some applications that are designed for Internet or Web communication automate much of the work. Both in and out of the application window, keyboard commands work pretty much the same. All of the communication with the remote host occurs "behind the scenes." Eudora, Outlook, and Netscape Communicator are examples of such applications. Each has its own advantages and limitations, and each accomplishes a relatively narrow range of tasks. If you're connecting to a machine that's running the Unix OS, and you're willing to learn the commands, direct communication with the Unix system can enable you to accomplish a variety of tasks without having to use multiple applications. The disadvantage, of course, is learning how to use Unix.

So far, we've looked at the software for computer systems and communication, as well as some types of computer networks. Now we'll explore some of the features of computer-mediated communication, and try to make sense of what we're doing when we point our Web browsers to particular Web "addresses."

Deciphering Web & E-Mail Addresses

Understanding a little about how the software and the hardware make things happen is a foundation for using the Web, but what about all those dots, dashes, and slashes in the Web addresses? Actually, Web and e-mail addresses are relatively simple, once you decode the system by which they're constructed.

Uniform Resource Locators for Web Sites (URLs)

First, let's look at a Uniform Resource Locator (URL—pronounced "Earl"), which is the formal name for a Web site address. All URLs are made up of similar components, and they all direct your Web browser (like Netscape or Microsoft Internet Explorer) to a hypertext document. You'll recall that the document is stored on a remote computer that's connected to the Web.

The first component of the URL is a series of several letters followed by a colon and two or three forward slashes:

```
http://
ftp://
gopher://
file:///
```

This component of the URL tells the Web browser what type of document is to be retrieved from the server. The most common type of document accessed with a browser is the Web page or html document, which is transferred using **h**ypertext **t**ransfer **p**rotocol (`http`). Secure pages for transmitting sensitive information such as credit card numbers sometimes appear as "`https`," which stands for **h**ypertext **t**ransfer **p**rotocol **s**ecure.

If the URL is preceded by "`ftp`," the browser will download a file using **f**ile **t**ransfer **p**rotocol. You also may see "`gopher`" preceding the URL, and the page will probably appear as a simple listing of file folders. That's because Gopher is an organizational and retrieval system that predates the Web for storing and accessing information through the Internet, that does not permit direct access into subdirectories. Finally, if you open a Web document (sometimes called an *html* document) that is stored on your own computer as a local file, a "`file`" prefix will appear in the URL, followed by the colon and *three* forward slashes.

The second segment of the URL signifies the "domain name" of the server from which a document can be retrieved by a Web browser. For example, `redcross.org` and `fullerton.edu` are the domain names for the American Red Cross and Cal State Fullerton. Domain names are the linguistic representations of one or several unique, numeric Internet Protocol (IP) addresses that exist nowhere else on the Internet. For example, the numeric IP address for `www.fullerton.edu` is 137.151.1.50, but of course, `www.fullerton.edu` is much easier to remember.

One advantage of the registered domain name for public relations is that the URL remains the same, even though the Web site may be moved from one server to another. This means that even if your client

moves its offices across the country and changes
ISPs, the same URL will remain usable. As we'll see
in Chapter 4, this is one way to add stability and
reliability to your clients' Internet messages.

When you set up a modem to connect with an Internet
Service Provider (ISP), you almost always need to
enter your ISP's numeric IP address in your software
setup. More than one computer may share a domain
name, but each computer must have a unique IP
address. The domain names in URLs appear
immediately after the first two forward slashes, and
often have a prefix like "www." Examples of URLs
comprising "www" prefixes and domain names
include:

```
http://www.usc.edu/
http://www.yahoo.com/
http://www.prsa.org/
```

Each domain name ends with a two- or three-letter
suffix that signifies the type of domain. In the United
States, domain name suffixes typically indicate the
nature of the organization that the name represents:

```
.com = commercial business
.edu = educational institution
.gov = government agency
.mil = military branch
.org = not-for-profit organization
```

Even if we knew nothing else about them, we would
be able to tell from the domain names listed above
that "usc" is an educational institution (the
University of Southern California), "yahoo" is a

commercial or corporate entity, and "`prsa`" is a not-for-profit organization.

In a similar vein, countries outside the United States are represented by two-character suffixes such as `.au` for Australia, `.ca` for Canada, `.de` for Denmark, and `.th` for Thailand. The URL for the University of Sydney, for example, is:

```
http://www.usyd.edu.au/
```

Often, this portion of the URL also includes an identifier that the host "server" computer is designated as a Web server. The domain name "`microsoft.com`," for example, may be preceded by "www" in the URL. In fact, the URL for the Microsoft Web site is:

```
http://www.microsoft.com/
```

Similarly, the URL for Purdue University is:

```
http://www.purdue.edu/
```

The slashes at the end of the three URLs listed above indicate that your Web browser will access the top level of a directory or a default html document that has been established by the system administrators at the University of Sydney, Microsoft, and Purdue. It's always a good idea to end the URL with a forward slash, since some systems will not accept URLs without either the slash or a file name extension (which is described in the next section).

Longer URLs typically designate the paths through directories that the browser must track to find a particular document. Each slash represents a new directory or folder. Take, for example, the following URL:

```
http://commfaculty.fullerton.edu/dwitmer/Syllabi.html
```

The domain name in this URL represents an IP address where directories for all faculty in the School of Communications at Cal State Fullerton are housed:

```
commfaculty.fullerton.edu
```

The default document that appears when the URL is typed as "`http://commfaculty.fullerton.edu/`" is a listing of faculty in the School of Communications. The next section of the URL is a directory or folder that has been designated with the name "`dwitmer`." That directory contains many different types of files created or stored by Diane Witmer. The last section specifies one particular file that the Web browser is to access—in this case, a document that lists course syllabi entitled "`Syllabi.html`."

Web files typically have three- or four-letter suffixes, much like the domain name suffixes. In the case of files, though, the suffixes designate the type of file to be accessed. We'll address file suffixes more thoroughly later in this chapter, but for now, it is useful to note that the "`.html`" suffix tells the Web browser to look for an html document. At this point, it is also is important to recognize that the directory dwitmer (in which files are held that are viewable to the world through Web browsers) constitutes a Web site. The document, "`Syllabi.html`," is a Web page on that site.

Tip: When typing a URL, it is important to type upper-case and lower-case letters exactly as listed in the URL because upper- and lower-case letters are read as separate characters by the host computers.

E-Mail Addresses

E-mail addresses typically consist of a user's login name, an @ sign, and the domain name where the e-mail account is held. Thus, Diane Witmer's e-mail address at California State University, Fullerton is:

```
dwitmer@fullerton.edu.
```

In this example, "dwitmer" is the login name, and "fullerton.edu" is the domain name for Cal State Fullerton. Note that in this example, the login name, dwitmer, also appears in the corresponding URL and is the name of the directory in which all of Witmer's html files are held:

```
http://commfaculty.fullerton.edu/dwitmer/
```

Chapter Summary

This chapter described the ways in which computers communicate. The computer operating systems manage computer files and applications, and computers with different operating systems can communicate through specialized hardware and software protocols. Computers may be used to do work independently, or they may be networked for collaboration and file sharing. Local Area Networks cover very limited physical spaces, while Wide Area

Networks cover large geographical areas. The largest WAN known is the Internet.

The World Wide Web is a specially designated system of servers throughout the Internet on which hypertext documents are stored. The Web enables users to move from point to point non-sequentially, and to access files in a variety of formats.

E-mail addresses and URLs are based on domain names, which represent servers at specific IP addresses. URLs specify the type of document to be retrieved, the domain name, and the directory path.

Exercises

1. Explore the software on your computer.

   What type and what version operating system
   does it have? If you're on an IBM-compatible, OS
   information appears as you start the computer. On
   a Mac, you can find the information in the Apple
   menu while the computer is running.

   What applications are loaded on the computer?
   Check the "Start" menu on Windows. On a Mac,
   use the Apple System Profiler in the Apple Menu.

2. If you don't already have a Telnet application or
   "client" on your computer, you'll need to
   download and install one to complete the
   following exercise.

   ## Preparation

   To download a client: If you're using an IBM-
   compatible computer, try NetTerm, which is a
   shareware program that you can download and
   tryout at no cost. If you're using a Macintosh
   computer, you can download NCSA Telnet,
   which is freeware. Both are available at:

   ```
   http://www.download.com/
   ```

Exercise

Try using a Telnet application to perform a library
search through CARL Uncover. You can get to
CARL Uncover three different ways. The first
way is to point your Web browser to:

```
telnet://database.carl.org/
```

Your telnet application should launch
automatically after the CARL Uncover server is
contacted and a window should appear on your
screen similar to the Telnet window in Figure 1.3.

The second way to reach the CARL site is to type
the following URL into your Web browser:

```
http://uncweb.carl.org/
```

At the Uncover Web site, click on the button for
"Telnet Access." Your Telnet client should launch
automatically and a window should appear on
your screen similar to the Telnet window in
Figure 1.3.

The last way to reach the site is to use the
"connect" menu in your telnet application to go
directly to:

```
uncweb.carl.org
```

Telnet allows only text (American Standard Code
for Information Exchange or "ASCII") data, so
you won't see any pretty graphics—but you'll see
a lot of words!

Note the menu commands within the Telnet window. Move from the Telnet window to the desktop and back to the Telnet window. **You can exit your Telnet session at any time with the `//exit` command.** *Caution*: **Be careful that you do not accidentally exit your browser or Windows!**

Follow the menu commands to search for or titles or authors.

References

Internet.com LLC. (1999). *PC Webopaedia.*
Available:
http://www.pcwebopaedia.com/

Lawler, J. M. (1995). *Metaphors We Compute By.* A
Lecture delivered to staff of the Informational
Technology Division of the University of Michigan.
Available:
http://www.virtualschool.edu/mon/Academia/Metaphors.html

Leiner, B. M., Cerf, V. G., Clark, D. D., Kahn, R. E.,
Kleinrock, L., Lynch, D. C., Postel, J., Roberts, L. G.,
& Wolff, S. (1998, February). *A Brief History of the
Internet.* Available:
http://www.isoc.org/internet-history/brief.html

Nelson, T. H. (1981/1990). *Literary Machines:
Report on and of project Xanadu, concerning word
processing, electronic publishing, hypertext,
thinkertoys, tomorrow's intellectual revolution, and
certain other topics including knowledge, education,
and freedom.* Swarthmore, Pa.: Self-
published/Sausalito, CA: Mindful Press. Portions of
the latest version (93.1) Available:
http://www.sfc.keio.ac.jp/~ted/TN/PUBS/LM/LMpage.htm

Chapter 2. Overview of Public Relations

Process and Theory

Learning Objectives

This chapter provides you first with an overview of public relations process and theory, then describes a systems model for public relations and organizations. Topics covered in the next pages include:

➤ The four-step public relations process.
➤ General systems theory.
➤ Implications of systems theory for public relations.

The Four-Step Public Relations Process

Nearly every public relations text describes the process of PR in about four basic steps. Although the specific terms vary, nearly all sources agree on the essence of the process as first proposed by Scott M. Cutlip, dean emeritus of The University of Georgia. For simplicity and consistency, this text adopts the language that the Public Relations Society of America uses to describe the four-step process: 1) Research, 2) Planning, 3) Execution, and 4) Evaluation. The next few chapters will describe some ways in which the Internet can be used during each phase.

It's important to note that although the public relations process is described as four discrete steps, each step is, in fact, constantly reiterated throughout any public relations campaign or program. During the planning phase, for example, research beyond that done in the first step may be necessary. Similarly, it may be necessary to fine-tune a public relations plan during the execution phase. As a result, the practitioner should not consider any particular step fully "finished" at any point during the process. The key, here, is to remember that a systematic approach is necessary for the ultimate success of any public relations endeavor.

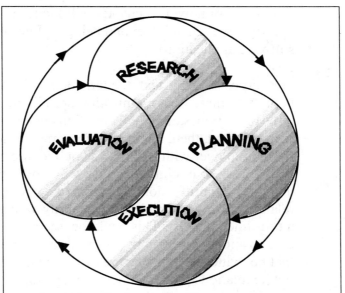

Figure 2.1. The four-step public relations process.
Research is the first step upon which each additional step
is built. Each step may be revisited at any time during the
process. Evaluation forms the basis for research in future
public relations campaigns and programs.

In this chapter, we'll briefly examine each step of the
pubic relations process in turn. First, however, we
need to set some semantic ground rules.

A Word about Words...

Because some widely used terms can take on a
variety of very specific meanings in the practice of
public relations, it is useful to lay out some
definitions. We speak of goals, objectives, strategies,
and tactics, but what does all that mean? The next
section of this chapter will define and illustrate the
terms "goals," "objectives," "strategies," and

"tactics." For now, this chapter will focus on what constitutes a "client" (beyond being an Internet software application).

For purposes of this text, the term "client" is used broadly to mean any organization or individual that hires the services of a public relations practitioner or firm. A client, then, might be a corporate or not-for-profit employer with an in-house public information department, or it might an organization or individual that hires the professional services of a public relations firm, or it might be a celebrity who employs a full-time publicist. This book focuses primarily on organizational clients, but it's important to remember that no matter what the nature of the client is, the public relations process of research, planning, execution, and evaluation is the same.

Research

Every good public relations program begins with an assessment of the client's needs, target publics, reputation, and current status within its environment. In this step of the public relations process, the practitioner defines the public relations problem, determines what has been done to date, and figures out what communication goals will best support the overall organizational goals. This means the practitioner must become an expert on a broad range of topics that are important to the client. Examples of the types of things that must be learned include details about the client's product or services, its competitive position in the marketplace, its stance on political or sensitive issues, the characteristics of its employees, and the demographics, values, lifestyles, and attitudes of its target publics.

The research and evaluation stages of the four-step process are something like matching bookends. Some of the research, for example, may serve as a baseline study that helps determine the effectiveness of a campaign during the evaluation step.

Planning

Once the public relations problem has been defined, the second stage of the public relations process is laying out the way the proposed campaign or program will unfold. During this phase, the practitioner establishes specific goals and objectives that will support the overall goals of the client, develops timelines and budgets, and determines the particular strategies and tactics that will serve the client's needs.

Similar to some of the research done in the first step, the measurements and criteria established during second, planning step help the practitioner determine the overall effectiveness of the campaign, both before and after its execution. Table 2.1 lists some brief definitions and examples of goals, objectives, strategies, and tactics.

Execution

The execution stage of the four-step process is sometimes also called the communication or programming stage. This is the phase during which specific messages are created and distributed through the appropriate channels, based on the information gathered during the research step and according to the objectives established during the planning step. In other words, the campaign or program is *implemented* or *executed* in light of the due dates, budgets, and other objectives that were established during the planning phase in order to communicate effectively with targeted publics. Many of the objectives, once executed, also serve as ways in which the overall campaign or program can be evaluated.

Evaluation

The final step of the public relations process, evaluation, often becomes the first step in a subsequent campaign or program. Careful evaluation of all phases of a program or campaign helps the practitioner determine how public relations activities can be improved in the future. This is the time to ask such questions as how well the deadlines that were established during the planning phase were met, whether materials were produced within the established budgets, the extent to which targeted publics received or accepted the message, and if the stated goals were achieved. This last question addresses if the plan was adequately detailed and the extent to which the overall program can be judged successful.

Term	Definition	Hypothetical Example: American Cancer Society
Goal	Something to be accomplished over a period of time. May be quite broad, or may be well focused.	Organizational goal: eradicate cancer. Organizational goal: prevent skin cancer. PR goal: Increase public awareness of the correlation between sun exposure and skin cancer.
Objective	Any activity that supports the goal. Must be *specific, measurable,* and *bound by time.* Must indicate progress toward achieving the goal. Often forms the basis for timelines and budget.	Conduct a campaign that will increase public awareness by 10% as measured by pre- and post-campaign surveys, no later than December of the following year. (There may be *sub*-objectives, too, such as creating ten 60-second PSAs by January 1)
Strategy	Overall unifying approach to achieving stated goals, such as decisions to target certain publics, timing, use of a common theme between different key messages to various target publics, etc.	Target youth. Focus on beauty instead of health. Equate tanning of skin with tanning of leather.
Tactic	When, where, how to complete the objectives and which tools or media to use.	Kicking off the campaign with a spring fashion show to tie in with swimsuit fashions. Sample message: "Skin that's tanned is leather."

Table 2.1. Thumbnail definitions & examples of goals, objectives, strategies, & tactics.

The four-step process is essential to public relations, but doesn't provide all the information that's needed for excellence in practice. We also need some perspective for understanding the context in which public relations occurs, the complexities of communication patterns, and the role that public

relations plays in and around organizations. One way
to do this is by using general systems theory.

General Systems Theory

Many public relations researchers find systems theory
helpful in illuminating the practice of PR. Therefore,
it's useful to look at the general characteristics of
systems and of systems theory as it concerns social
relationships.

First proposed by biologist Ludwig von Bertalanffy,
general systems theory has evolved into an academic
field of its own. One of the major advantages of
systems theory is that it accounts for complex
behaviors and relationships between system parts.

Definition and Characteristics of Systems

In general, we can define systems as interrelated sets
of things that create a unique entity. These
interrelated things are called system *components*.
Systems also function within their immediate
surroundings or *environment*, although not all
systems are particularly sensitive to environmental
influences. As a result, systems are categorized
according to their relative openness to environment.

Open systems constantly strive to survive by
responding to environmental forces that act on them
and to maintain a healthy balance or *homeostasis*
between input and output. A *cybernetic* system is the

most *open* of open systems, a term that refers to the relative sensitivity of a system to its environment. A cybernetic system is sensitive to environmental influences, and includes internal mechanisms that allow it to adapt to environmental changes. An example of a cybernetic system is the human body, which senses heat and cold, and makes internal adjustments to maintain a reasonably constant core temperature. A closed system, on the other hand, is, as the name implies, closed from environmental influences. An example of a closed system is a key-wound clock, which neither recognizes nor adjusts for external influences.

Open systems utilize resources from the environment as *input*, transform those resources during *throughput*, and produce an *output* of some sort. Biological systems, for example, use nutrients to produce energy and waste. Figure 2.2 illustrates a simple model of a *generic system.*

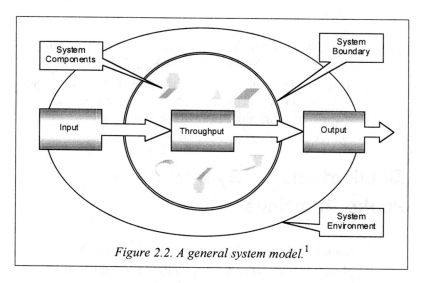

Figure 2.2. A general system model.[1]

Systems are generally considered hierarchical, in that their components may also be systems. This means that the definition of what constitutes a system is pretty much arbitrary, and depends on the particular area of interest. Looking again at the biological example, consider the circulation of a plant or animal, which occurs within the circulatory *system*. The plant or animal within which it resides is the immediate environment or the *suprasystem*. Circulatory system components are bounded by the vessels through which the blood (or in the case of plants, xylem) flows, and the cells that make up the blood are components of the circulatory system.

The circulatory system is a *subsystem* or component of a larger biological system—a plant or an animal. Similarly, the components of a circulatory system are bona fide systems in their own rights. Cells, for example, are systems in which the components are organelles such as mitochondria, ribosomes, and nuclei.

It's easy to see how systems theory can apply to computers and computer networks, but how does it apply to communication? The answer is easier to see when we consider relationships between people, groups, and organizations as social systems.

Implications of Systems Theory for Public Relations

Social systems, such as organizations, use resources of goods and services to produce output of new goods and services. They also typically have permeable

boundaries, in that environmental elements constantly
enter and leave them. We each live, work, and play in
a variety of social systems, including churches,
schools, businesses, and clubs. We join them, we
abandon them, we are hired into them, and we
graduate from them. In each case, we influence them
even as they influence us.

The public relations practitioner acts as a boundary
spanner in organizational systems. Environmental
scanning brings information into the organization,
and external communications send information into
the organizational environment. Therefore, public
relations serves a feedback function that helps the
client systems interpret their environments in order to
maintain homeostasis.

Beyond a functional understanding of the public
relations role, systems theory has undergirded a good
deal of research to advance the field. James Grunig of
the University of Maryland, with Todd Hunt of
Rutgers, The University of New Jersey, developed a
four-model overview of public relations, which is
grounded in a systems perspective of the boundary
spanning and feedback roles of public relations in
organizations. Their models describe historical
emphases of public relations practices, and focus
largely on one-way versus two-way communication
between the public relations client and its target
publics. The Press Agentry/Publicity model and
Public Information models both rely on one-way
transmission of messages; the Two-Way
Asymmetrical and Two-Way Symmetrical models
rely on two-way transmission of information.
However, the purposes of each of the four models are
very different. The Press Agentry/Publicity model at

one end of the spectrum has a propagandistic goal of advocacy, and is not particularly concerned with truth in the message. The Two-Way Symmetrical model at the other end of the spectrum has a mediational goal of mutual understanding, and truth is a key consideration. Clearly, these models have both functional and ethical implications for the practice of public relations.

Chapter Summary

This chapter offered a brief overview of a widely used process and perspective of public relations. It described an iterative, four-step public relations process of research, planning, execution, and evaluation. In the research step, the public relations problem is defined and information is gathered about the client, its goals, it target publics, its products or services, and what needs to be done. During the planning step, the practitioner establishes goals and measurable objectives in order to set timelines, budgets, and criteria for evaluation. In the execution step, the practitioner develops and disseminates the messages for the campaign or program. Finally, the evaluation step allows the practitioner to reflect on the success of the public relations endeavor and to develop ways in which the next campaign might be improved.

Much of the research that has helped advance the field of public relations has been conducted from a systems perspective. Systems theory views relationships between people and organizations as social systems. Open systems are sensitive to environmental influences and transform input from the environment into output. The role of public relations in systems is one of boundary spanner that enables the system to adapt to its environment in order to maintain homeostasis.

Up to this point, this text has described the process and theory of public relations. In the next chapter, it will look at communication models and identify the role of feedback in the communication process. Then it will examine the extent to which systems theory helps us understand public relations in the electronic environment.

Exercises

1. You've been asked to help launch the opening of a new Chinese restaurant in your hometown. What is the first thing you would do? What research might you need to do?

2. Draw a diagram of your computer system. What is its boundary? What are the components? What would you consider its immediate environment? Can you consider your computer system a component in a larger suprasystem? Why or why not?

3. Think about your class or office as a social system. What is the suprasystem? What are the components? Are the components made up of still more components? Are there larger systems in which the suprasystem resides? What is the social boundary? Is it permeable? Be sure to provide a rationale for your answers.

References

Athey, T. H. (1982). *Systematic systems approach: An integrated method for solving systems problems.* New Jersey: Prentice-Hall.

Von Bertalanffy, L. (1968). *General systems theory.* New York: Braziller

Cutlip, S. M., & Center, A. H. (1952). *Effective public relations: Pathways to public favor.* New York: Prentice-Hall.

Cutlip, S. M., Center, A. H., & Broom, G. M. (1994). *Effective public relations.* (7th ed.). Englewood Cliffs, NJ: Prentice-Hall.

Grunig, J. E. (1992). *Excellence in public relations and communication management.* Hillsdale, NJ: Lawrence Erlbaum.

Grunig, J. E. & Hunt, T. T (1984). *Managing public relations.* New York: Holt, Rinehart and Winston.

Hunt, T., & Grunig, J. E. (1994). *Public relations techniques.* Fort Worth: Harcourt Brace.

Kendall, R. (1996). *Public relations campaign strategies.* New York: HarperCollins.

Nager, N. R., & Allen, T. H. (1984). *Public relations: Management by objectives.* New York: Longman.

Wilcox, D. L., Ault, P. H., & Agee, W. K. (1998).
Public relations: Strategies and tactics. New York:
Addison Wesley Longman.

Notes

[1] Model adapted from Athey, T. H. (1982). Systematic systems approach: An integrated method for solving systems problems. New Jersey: Prentice-Hall.

Chapter 3. Overview of Computer-Mediated Communication

Process and Theory

Learning Objectives

This chapter provides you first with an overview of the communication process, and then develops a model of computer-mediated communication. Finally, it addresses the ways in which communication is both enabled and constrained by technology, and offers a theoretical grounding for the practice of public relations on the Internet. Key topics covered in the next pages include:

- ➢ Basic models of communication.
- ➢ Synchronous and asynchronous forms of communication
- ➢ A mechanistic model of computer-mediated communication.
- ➢ Theories of structuration and adaptive structuration.
- ➢ Computer-mediated communication as both medium and outcome of the public relations process.

Basic Models of Communication

Now that we've reviewed the process of public relations, we're almost ready to look at the ways in which we can use the Internet for each step of the process. First, though, it's important to think of the Internet as a mode of communication, in order to understand how public relations communications might both avoid the pitfalls and take advantage of computer-based technology. To begin, this chapter looks at two general categories of communication, then at some basic models of human communication. Finally, it explores the extent to which communication models help us understand computer-mediated communication.

Simultaneous & Nonsimultaneous Communication

Communication, especially computer-mediated communication, is often thought of in terms of the relationship between the parties involved in the communication. The concept is sometimes termed synchronous and asynchronous communication. T. Andrew Finn of the University of Kentucky uses the terms *simultaneous* and *nonsimultaneous*. Finn's rationale is that *synchronous* and *asynchronous* are terms that have very particular meanings in information systems and telecommunications parlance, which could generate semantic confusion in a field that already has more than its share of confusion. For that reason, this text adopts his language of simultaneous and nonsimultaneous communication.

Simultaneous communication (sometimes called synchronous communication) occurs when the parties involved are engaged at the same moment in the communication process. Face-to-face interactions, telephone conversations, and online chat rooms are examples of simultaneous communication. *Nonsimultaneous* (or asynchronous) *communication* does not require the communicators to be engaged in the process at the same time. Examples of nonsimultaneous communication include e-mail, "snail" mail, bulletin boards, Usenet[1] newsgroups, and the World Wide Web.

The differences between simultaneous and nonsimultaneous forms of communication are important to us because they each provide different opportunities and challenges. If, for example, you want people to have instant access to a live human being for immediate response to technical problems, you should to consider simultaneous communication, such as a telephone hotline or a chat room with an online expert logged on. If, on the other hand, you want to reduce labor intensive one-on-one responses to commonly asked questions, nonsimultaneous communication is a better choice. Here, you might use such tools as an online "Frequently Asked Questions" (FAQ) file that asks and answers commonly asked questions about your organization or product, or a newsgroup where an expert can monitor messages and post answers to questions that arise. Of course, making those decisions depends on both a clear understanding of the nature of computer-

mediated communication and of the general
communication process.

Both simultaneous and nonsimultaneous group
discussions tend to create "cybercommunities" in
which members develop strong feelings about their
online cultures, norms, and values. It's therefore
critical that the newcomer "lurk" (the term used for
reading but not posting to public discussions on the
Internet) for a while before jumping into a
conversation. Strong rebukes, often in the form of
"flames" (insults or worse), tend to befall the
unwitting violator of group norms on the Internet. It's
therefore always a good idea to seek out the FAQ of a
new group and to "lurk" for a while before posting to
the group population.

Mechanistic Models of Human Communication

Public relations practitioners frequently refer to their
work in terms of sending messages through channels
to targeted recipients. This terminology stems from
what Aubrey Fisher called a "mechanistic
perspective," which views communication as
conveying or transporting meaning across space and
time. Figure 3.1 depicts a simple mechanistic model
of communication.

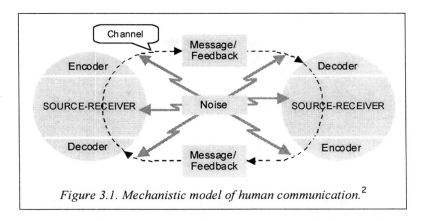

Figure 3.1. Mechanistic model of human communication.[2]

Because human communication usually is symbolic, a *source* or sender must first encode a thought or idea into symbolic form then send the resulting *message* through some sort of conveyance or *channel* to a receiver. Both the source and the receiver may be a person, a group, or an organization. The channel by which the message is sent may be auditory (such as a recited speech), visual (such as using a blackboard to illustrate the speech), or any other medium or combination of media that can convey meaning to the recipient. These examples, of course, imply that multiple channels may be used to convey a single message.

Most communication is two-way, in that it involves *feedback* or some sort of return communication from the recipient. This means that the receiver is a source of communication—and by the same token, the source is also a receiver. However, communication does not always convey meaning precisely as intended because *noise* can interfere with its transmission or reception. Just as static or snow on a television disrupts the picture, a variety of things can disrupt effective communication. Noise can be internal to the sender or the receiver, or it can be external to the communication effort. If a room is too warm, if a communicator is distracted by personal problems, if someone else is shouting a competing message, or if cultural differences render the perceptions and understandings of recipient and sender incompatible, noise has interfered with the communication process.

Noise is not the only thing that might interfere with the intention of communication. Public relations practitioners also are concerned with *gatekeepers*. The gatekeeping function is one of filtering or selecting messages in some way between the source and receiver. An example of a gatekeeper is the newspaper editor who decides which articles will appear in the paper and which will never see print. This places the gatekeeper squarely in the middle of our communication model as a third receiver-source.

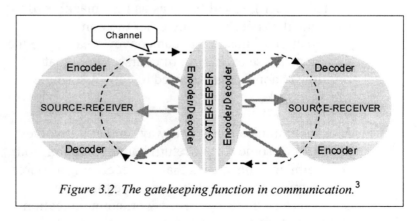

Figure 3.2. The gatekeeping function in communication.[3]

For the public relations practitioner, the gatekeeper represents a layered segmentation of target publics. As you might note in Figure 3.2, the gatekeeper must decode received messages, then re-encode them before (and if) they are sent to the ultimate recipient.

This means the PR person formulate messages with the gatekeeper as well as the ultimate recipient in mind. For example, the practitioner must write a news release for the newspaper editor in order to use the editor's newspaper a channel to reach the intended audience. The editor must decode the release in order to determine if it is newsworthy and appropriate to the newspaper's readership. As a result, the release must demonstrate newsworthiness, timeliness, proximity, and other characteristics of acceptable news. Once the release is accepted, the editor then re-encodes it for print, perhaps to the extent of rewriting it as a newspaper article. The newspaper reader, then, ultimately reads articles that have been through a translation process, of sorts.

This second model of communication is a *mediated* model, because the gatekeeper serves as a mediator between sender and receiver. This brings us to the concept of computer-mediated communication.

A Mechanistic Model of Computer-Mediated Communication

Chapter 1 described hardware and software systems that make CMC possible. This chapter examines more closely the process of CMC. As the name implies, computer-mediated communication may be thought of as having a gatekeeper or even a series of gatekeepers. Of course, most gatekeepers in CMC are computers rather than people, but in terms of message transmission between source and receiver, the function is similar. The message must be prepared in a manner that is suitable and acceptable to the

intermediary computers before it will successfully
reach its destination. Here, then, is a combination of
human and technological gatekeepers, each of which
may require a conceptual or technological process for
message transmission. That means any
communication that occurs through computers may
go through a complex series of transmissions ,
decodings, re-encodings, and retransmissions before
it is completed.

Consider, for example, a simple e-mail exchange
between two people who live within five miles of
each other, whom we'll call John and Mary. First,
Mary must have some idea of what she wants to
communicate to John. That means she must first have
a concept that she can both bring to consciousness
and encode into symbolic form—in this case, written
American English. She then must enter the message
into her computer, and she must do it in a format that
both her desktop computer and her e-mail software
application can accept. Fortunately for Mary, this
usually means simply typing the message; the
computer and its software handle the rest of the
encoding process to prepare the message for
transmission. Then Mary hits a "send" button and
voila! If John is logged onto his e-mail account, he
can receive Mary's message in a matter of seconds.
But what happened to Mary's message between the
time that she keyed it in and the time that John read
it? Quite a bit, as it happens.

Although Mary and John only see their e-mail
exchanges on their computer screens, all of their
messages are routed through several computers and
undergo a variety of transformations in the process.
First, Mary's message must be decoded and re-

encoded for transmission through some sort of data line. For a private home, this is usually a telephone line or a television cable. That means the message content must be transformed from digital data that the computer understands to analog data that a phone line can handle. That is the purpose of a modem. In fact, the word "modem" is really an abbreviated term that refers to "*mo*dulating and *dem*odulating" the data to and from digital and analog forms.

You can see that even before the information leaves her desktop, Mary's message has been decoded, accepted, re-encoded, and transmitted by its first two gatekeepers: her computer and her modem. It then is distributed through many other computers, some of which may be some distance away, before it reaches the computer that hosts John's e-mail account. To illustrate this point, the following list traces the route a message must travel between from a home computer to a host server that is located approximately five miles away. Each item in the list represents a different computer:

➤ Mary's computer and modem
  1. `cr2-hfc1.flrtn1.occa.home.net`
  2. `r1-fe0-0-100bt.bnapk1.occa.home.net`
  3. `10.0.242.5`
  4. `bb1.rdc1.sfba.home.net`
  5. `sl-gw5-sj-1-1-0-t3.sprintlink.net`
  6. `sl-bb10-sj-1-3-155m.sprintlink.net`
  7. `sl-bb21-stk-7-0.sprintlink.net`
  8. `sl-bb21-stk-8-0.sprintlink.net`
  9. `sl-gw11-stk-0-0-0.sprintlink.net`
  10. `sl-csuhay-1-0-0-t3.sprintlink.net`
  11. `sta-hay-atm.csu.net`
  12. `wested-sta-atm.csu.net`
  13. `ful-wested-atm.csu.net`
➤ Host server: student.fullerton.edu

This list of 13 "hops" depicts only the routing of
Mary's message to the host server where her e-mail
account is housed. It would be far longer if it also
outlined the route between her host server
(student.fullerton.edu) and John's host server
(assuming John's account is on a different host), then
traced the route from John's host server to his
personal computer. To complicate matters even
further, the message transmission also includes
additional modems between many of the intermediary
computers.

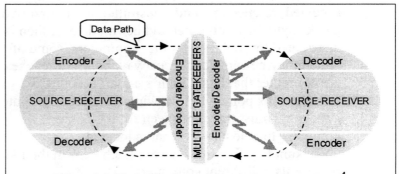

Figure 3.3. The multiple gatekeeping function in CMC.[4]
*The Data Path is the channel or channels through which the
information must travel, such as cable, telephone line, satellite, or
other form of transmission. The Source-Receivers represent the
originator(s) and recipient(s) of the communication message.*

It's easy to see from all this that our model of
communication can become quite complicated when
it's drawn to represent computer-mediated
communication. For simplicity's sake, Figure 3.3
depicts the gatekeeping function at only one
gatekeeping node, but as we've already demonstrated,
it's important to remember that CMC is characterized
by many gatekeeping nodes.

To complicate matters even further, as noted in Chapter 1, we don't interact only with each other in CMC. Our first and most immediate interaction is with keyboard, screen, and central processing unit (CPU). This means we're not merely using the technology as a conduit. Rather, we're communicating *with* as well as *through* the computers that are involved in our mediated human communications.

Donna L. Hoffman and Thomas P. Novak of Vanderbilt University are sensitive to the ways in which people interact with computers, as well as to the fact that Web sites, e-mail distribution lists, chat rooms, and other forms of CMC accommodate many source-receivers. Hoffman and Novak have proposed that in computer-mediated environments (CMEs), we need to rethink the traditional broadcast, one-to-many model as a multicast, many-to-many model. In fact, the one-to-many broadcast model is inadequate for CMC both because it does not account for the many-to-many relationships and because it implies a unidirectional flow of communication. Clearly, CMC is multidirectional on the Web, in Usenet newsgroups, and in e-mail distribution lists. As a result, our model of CMC becomes even more complex. Figure 3.4 depicts a greatly simplified multicast, multidirectional model of computer-mediated communication.

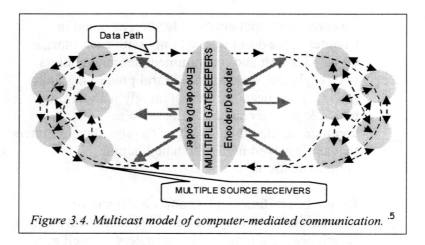

Figure 3.4. Multicast model of computer-mediated communication. [5]

As you might already have discerned from our exploration of CMC, our communications are both enabled and constrained by the technologies we use. We can use computers to collapse time and distance, but we also must make sure that our messages are compatible with the technological systems through which they travel. What's more, as we'll see in the next section, our communications both alter and are altered by technology and the ways in which we use it.

Understanding CMC from a Structuration Perspective

Traditional models of communication and systems are useful for putting names to various aspects of the process and role of public relations. However, they don't adequately address the nature of the relationships between the communicator, message, and channel. Communicating through technological means, in particular, makes understanding those relationships paramount to developing an overall understanding of the communication process. One perspective that can enable this is that of structuration.

Structuration theory, which has been advanced primarily through the work of Anthony Giddens, goes a step beyond general systems theory and frames human interactions as the ways in which our social structures are formed. Steve Banks and Patricia Riley have described four central concepts of structuration:

1. agency and reflexivity,
2. duality of structure,
3. practice and time/space "distanciation," and
4. integration and institutional reproduction.

The following sections briefly explore each of these four characteristics of structuration.

Agency & Reflexivity

First, structuration proposes that human agency or intentional action is possible through stocks of knowledge that are created through social exchanges. In other words, people know how to proceed in social interactions based on mutually understood norms and learning experiences. We reflect on those learning experiences, and that reflection allows us to express our goals and motivations, although not all actions are consciously motivated. This means, of course, that our social processes sometimes result in unintended consequences.

An example of agency and reflexivity can be seen in the classroom. We learn from many school experiences that certain classroom behaviors are expected of instructors, and that other behaviors are expected of students. As a result, we act accordingly when we're in a classroom setting.

Duality of Structure

Second, duality of structure refers to the idea that structural properties of social systems are the *medium* through which our interactions take place as well as the *outcome* of those interactions. In other words, we draw on structures to produce action, and those actions at the same time reinforce the structures upon which they are based. Of course, that means we need to know what structures are.

The concept of *structures* refers to the rules and resources that people use in social interactions. There are three basic types of structures: 1) legitimation, 2) domination, and 3) signification.

Legitimation, the first of the three structures, refers to normative action. We legitimize things (or don't) by the ways in which we behave toward them. In a business-related telephone conversation, for example, the accepted communicative pattern is to answer with either a "hello" or a self-introduction, after which the caller returns the salutation. This brief exchange enacts a social structure. If it is violated, one or both parties may feel uncertain how to proceed with the conversation. The structural features, in this case, include rules of turn-taking, norms, and self-identification, and they constitute both the product and constraint of the exchange. The second structure, domination, is concerned with distribution of power, or who has the *authority* and the *allocation* of resources that enable us to get things done. For example, the public relations department may have both the authority to contact the media and the resources to sponsor a press tour. However, it probably would not have the authority to negotiate a union contract. The third structure is signification, which refers primarily to the ways in which things are named, along with the myths, legends, and heroes social processes create. Joe DiMaggio's death, for example, signified in the American consciousness more than just the passing of a baseball great or Marilyn Monroe's husband. In the minds of many people, it also signified the loss of an icon that represented gentlemanly conduct and even heroism.

Giddens has described language and linguistics from a structuration perspective, and language offers a good example of the duality of structure. We can consider language as a system of rules (grammar and syntax) and resources (words, alphabet, and punctuation symbols). That means language is considered to be a social structure. We can speak to one another because we draw upon our rules and resources of grammar and vocabulary. By using those rules and resources, we help others understand what we are trying to say. At the same time, using appropriate grammar and vocabulary legitimizes and reinforces them as the rules and resources upon which we've based our communication. Therefore, the structures of language not only enabled us to converse, they were the *medium* of the conversation. At the same time, they were the outcome of the conversation because the rules of grammar and the resources of vocabulary were reinforced in the exchange.

Practice & Time/Space Distanciation

The third key concept of structuration is "distanciation" of time and space from practice. This means that structures exist only as people's remembrances across spans of time and geographic distances. Structures have no reality beyond the social interactions that create them. This means that while actions may occur in a particular place and at a particular time, the relationship between them and the ways in which they are reproduced stretch out across time and space, as stocks of knowledge upon which we constantly draw. A classroom meeting, for example, ceases to exist in time and space when its members go home, except within their memories. But class members reproduce classroom practices and expectations in their interactions with one another outside of the class meeting and in other classrooms.

Integration & Institutional Reproduction

Finally, social integration refers to the idea that social systems are interactive, and that social processes are reciprocal over time. As our knowledge and self-reflexivity enable our interactions, the structures we enact become embedded within our social systems. The structures that become most deeply embedded typically are the oldest and most durable, and they may become institutionalized. An example might be the administrative assistant who decides one morning to pick up the mail at the post office as a courtesy. She falls into the habit of swinging by the post office every day at 7:30 A.M., then distributing the mail throughout the office around 8:00 A.M. Over a period of time, then, her practice of going through the office with the mail becomes institutionalized so it is not only perceived to be the secretary's responsibility, but it is widely thought to be a formal part of the job description. This example illustrates not only the ways in which a practice might be institutionalized over time, but also the consequences, both intended and unintended, of our social interactions.

Implications of Structuration for CMC

Structuration is becoming an important perspective in the study of communication. It also is drawing attention from researchers as helpful for understanding the nature of computer-mediated communication. It's relatively easy to see that we draw on both technological rules (such as sending text-only e-mail) and resources (such as access to computer networks), as well as on social rules (such as e-mail "netiquette") and resources (such as keeping computer software current) in order to communicate with computers. Furthermore, structures of CMC, like those of language, are both the medium and the outcome of our communications. CMC both creates and is created by the nature of the technology, in bits, bytes, and nanoseconds—and that has implications for the ways in which public relations practitioners think about publics and public opinion in the electronic environment.

The Emergence of New Publics on the Internet

Internet technologies challenge public relations practitioners to redefine their target publics. The typology of publics that researchers most often use is drawn from James Grunig's situational theory of publics, which is grounded in a systems perspective of public relations. The situational theory views publics as "active" or "passive," and is significant because it centralizes the communication behavior of publics and public participation in public relations activities.

Situational theory helps us analyze various levels of a public's opinions and orientation toward issues, and it allows us to categorize or segment publics, then attempt to predict their communication behaviors. However, New Publics emerge online every day. In newsgroups, online bulletin boards, chat rooms and Listservs, New Publics form through members' shared interactions across time and space. People exchange ideas, feelings, and experiences based on mutual interests rather than geographic proximity. For example, Disney fans cluster in international newsgroups to discuss theme parks, movies, video releases, and collectibles. Similarly, users of various computer manufacturers congregate in Listservs and newsgroups that focus on system upgrades, improving processor speed, and peer support for technical problems. In other words, online communities create what Zoraida Cozier, a doctoral candidate at Purdue University, calls "New Publics" that can affect the client, and those New Publics shape both their online and offline communities as they share their experiences with friends, neighbors, coworkers, and Internet acquaintances.

Online publics are not isolated from each other or from other social systems in society. They interact with other people, influence each other, and bring new perspectives from their offline lives into their online communities. A structuration approach to understanding these New Publics can help practitioners understand the ways in which members of a public produce and reproduce social structures while, at the same time, allowing sensitivity to the interconnections between the public and its environments. This means that a structuration analysis of New Publics can help the practitioner determine a public's level of openness, its perspectives on and within interdependent organizations, and its possibility for creating other publics both offline and online. As a result, the practitioner can investigate the communicative practices of new online publics, and gain new insights into how to better understand and segment them.

Internet Users as Target Publics

Structuration also helps us understand the ways in which we might rethink our segmentation of New Publics. The technology allows us to tailor our messages to individuals rather than to massive audiences. Thus, we often target a public of one, rather than a particular demographic or psychographic segment. One example of this is the "cookie" technology that enables Web users to configure how and what they view on the Web sites they access.

Cookies are little strings of data that a host server attaches to a user's Web browser cache file. The data are saved on the user's computer. This enables functionality by the server whenever the user returns to the Web site where a cookie was set. For example, if you log into a Web site that welcomes you by your name whenever you visit, it is doing so because a cookie has been set in your Web browser's cache files that gives the host server the information.

Because cookies store data about the people who access our Web sites, they can help us learn who our target publics are, in terms of interests, values, and lifestyles, which, in turn, enables us to prepare and deliver messages directly to individuals. This means that, unlike a message in a printed newspaper, the viewer can avoid viewing items that are of marginal or no interest. For the public relations practitioner, this is both good and bad news. It's good news because we can target very specific messages to particular individuals. It's bad news because the Web user is less likely to browse our messages in passing. Either way, Internet technologies both create and are created through newly emerging interest groups and target publics.

Because the social processes of New Publics occur in a technological environment, it is important to understand the ways in which the technology both constrains and enables their communication. *Adaptive structuration* is useful in that regard, because it takes into consideration the mutual influences of technology and group social interactions.

Adaptive Structuration

The concept of adaptive structuration was developed by Marshall Scott Poole of Texas A&M University and Gerardine DeSanctis of Duke University through their research in group decision support systems (GDSSs). Adaptive structuration, as the name implies considers how groups adapt the structures (for example, the rules of voting procedures and the resources of databases) of GDSSs through their social processes.

Adaptive structuration focuses on two aspects of technological systems—the *structural features* and the *spirit*. Structural features are built into the system. They are the specific rules and resources that operate in a group. The *spirit* of a system is the principle that holds its rules and resources together and represents the general goals of the system.

Systems both reproduce and are reproduced through group interactions. That means they can be influenced by both the technological and social contexts in which they function. As a result, people may *faithfully* appropriate systems in ways that were intended or *ironically* appropriate them in ways that were not intended. Figure 3.5 represents an overview of adaptive structuration.

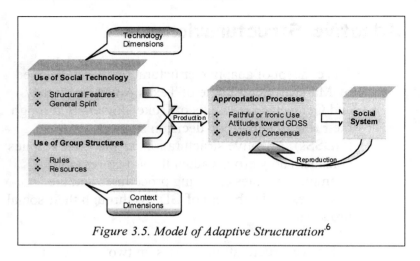

Figure 3.5. Model of Adaptive Structuration[6]

To take this description of adaptive structuration from GDSSs to e-mail, consider the organization that installs an e-mail system with the intent to increase speed and efficiency of communication between employees. The structures of the system are the same for any e-mail system. The spirit is the increase in efficiency and ease of reaching fellow employees without having to wait until schedules permit person-to-person contact. The employees may use the system faithfully, as it was intended. However, a group of disgruntled employees circumvents the traditional chain of command by writing a chain letter to their supervisor and copying the CEO. This illustrates an ironic appropriation of the system.

The concepts of both structural duality and of system reciprocity and integration are evident in adaptive structuration. Both the social system and the technological system mutually produce and are produced by one another. This has major implications for the practice of public relations.

Chapter Summary

This chapter presented an overview of the process of communication and outlined several basic communication models that are widely used in the practice of public relations practitioners. Simultaneous communication occurs when the communicators are engaged in the process at the same time, such as in a telephone conversation. Nonsimultaneous communication occurs when the communicators are not engaged at the same time, such as leaving and reading messages on a bulletin board.

The mechanistic model of communication concerns transmission of a message through a channel or several channels from a sender-receiver to a receiver-sender. Internal or external factors can create noise that interferes with the communication process. A gatekeeper controls the flow of communications between sender-receiver and receiver-sender. The gatekeeping function is one of mediation, and is present in computer-mediated communication. CMC consists of many gatekeepers, both technological and human. Because CMC accommodates many source-receivers, a many-to-many multicast model is more appropriate than a traditional one-to-many broadcast model.

Structuration and adaptive structuration help us understand how the technology and the social interactions both create and are created through CMC. The three basic structures outlined in structuration theory are legitimation (normative action), domination (allocation and authorization of resources), and signification (the naming of things).

Duality of structure is a key concept of structuration that facilitates understanding of CMC as both medium and outcome of the public relations process.

Structuration enables public relations practitioners to rethink how they target publics both through and as a result of emergent Internet technologies. New online publics are created through the medium, and the practitioner can now prepare and deliver messages to target publics of single individuals.

Exercises

1. You are the new public relations director for a utility company. Your boss has asked you to write the copy for some bill stuffers to explain a new pricing structure to utility consumers.

   a) Who is the sender-receiver?
   b) Who is the receiver-sender?
   c) What is the message?
   d) What is the channel?
   e) What noise might interfere with the communication?
   f) What feedback might you expect and through what channels?
   g) Is there a gatekeeper involved? Justify your answer.

2. Use the model template below to identify and label the elements of the communication process.

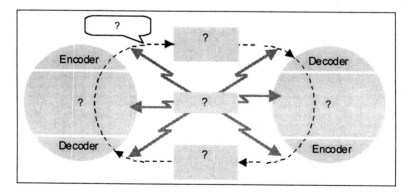

3. Reflect on our discussion of noise in the mechanistic model of communication. If someone were to call you at this moment, what factors

(both internal and environmental) would
constitute noise in your telephone
communication?

4. Think about an organization to which you belong.
    It might be your religious group or your business
    or favorite club or a sports team or a charity.
    What structures of legitimation, signification, and
    domination can you identify? Be sure to explain
    your answers.

References

Baym, N. (1998) The Emergence of On-line Community. In Steven Jones (Ed.) *Cybersociety 2.0: Revisiting computer-mediated communication and community* (pp. 35-68), Newbury Park, CA: Sage.

Cozier, Z. R. & Witmer, D. F. (in press) The development of a structuration analysis of New Publics in an electronic environment. In R. Heath & G. Vasquez, (Eds.). *Handbook of public relations.* Newbury Park, CA: Sage.

Finn, T. A. (1998, July). *A conceptual framework for organizing communication and information systems.* Paper presented to the annual conference of the International Communication Association, Jerusalem, Israel.

Fisher, B. A. (1978). *Perspectives on human communication.* New York: Macmillan

Giddens, A. (1979). *Central problems in social theory: Action, structure, and contradiction.* Berkeley, CA: University of California Press.

Giddens, A. (1984). *The constitution of society: Outline of the theory of structuration.* Berkeley, CA: University of California Press.

Grunig, J. E. (1989). Publics, audiences and market segments: Segmentation principles for campaigns. In C. T. Salmon (Ed.), *Information Campaigns: Balancing social values and social change* (pp.199-228). CA: Sage.

Grunig, J. E., & Repper, F. C. (1992). Strategic
Management, Publics, and Issues. In J. E. Grunig
(Ed.), *Excellence in public relations and
communication management* (pp. 117-159) Hillsdale,
NJ: Lawrence Erlbaum.

Hoffman, D. L., & Novak, T. P. (1996), Marketing in
computer-mediated environments: Conceptual
foundations. *Journal of Marketing, 60.* 50-68.

McLaughlin, M. L., Osborne, K. K., & Smith, C. B.
(1995). Standards of conduct on Usenet. In S. Jones
(Ed.), *Cybersociety: Computer-Mediated
Communication and Communit.* (pp. 90-111).
Thousand Oaks, CA: Sage.

Poole, M. S., & DeSanctis, G. (1989). Understanding
the use of group decision support systems: The theory
of adaptive structuration. In J. Fulk, & C. Steinfield
(Eds.), *Organization and communication technology*
(pp. 173-193). Newbury Park, CA: Sage.

Westley, B. H., & MacLean, Jr., M. S. (1957). A
conceptual model for communication research.
Journalism Quarterly, 34. 31-38.

Wilcox, D. L., Ault, P. H., & Agee, W. K. (1998).
Public relations: Strategies and tactics. New York:
Addison Wesley Longman.

Notes

[1] Usenet is a distributed electronic bulletin board system (BBS) that resides on a large network of computers connected to the Internet.

[2] Model adapted from Fisher, B. A. (1978). *Perspectives on human communication*. New York: Macmillan, p. 108.

[3] Model adapted from Fisher, B. A. (1978). *Perspectives on human communication*. New York: Macmillan, p. 118.

[4] Model adapted from Fisher, B. A. (1978). *Perspectives on human communication*. New York: Macmillan, p. 118.

[5] Model adapted from Fisher, B. A. (1978). *Perspectives on human communication*. New York: Macmillan, p. 118.

[6] Model adapted from Poole, M. S., & DeSanctis, G. (1989). Understanding the use of group decision support systems: The theory of adaptive structuration. In J. Fulk, & C. Steinfield (Eds.), *Organization and communication technology* (p. 182). Newbury Park, CA: Sage.

Chapter 4. Research

The First Step

Learning Objectives

This chapter addresses research, the first step of the four-step process, within the context of the Internet. This chapter covers both the process of doing research on the Internet and the research that's required for developing a Web presence. Major topics covered in the next few pages include:

➤ Strategies for conducting secondary research on the Internet.
➤ Five types of search systems.
➤ Seven searching techniques supported by search systems.
➤ Developing keywords and search terms.
➤ Discerning the quality of information on the Internet.
➤ Advantages and challenges of research on the Internet.
➤ What you need to know before you develop your client's Web presence.

Thinking about the Research Approach

Any public relations endeavor begins with research. It may be primary research in which we gather, analyze, and report the data, or it may be secondary research, which is gathered and archived by someone else. Looking up statistics in a library database is an example of secondary research. Conducting a survey of readers' interests for a magazine is an example of primary research.

A fair amount of both primary and secondary research can be done through the Internet, but it's a good idea to keep in mind the advantages and limitations of the medium. Webs, after all, are characterized by having many threads that go in many different directions—and those threads can enmesh and shroud the unsuspecting traveler. Therefore, in this chapter, we'll look first at some techniques for conducting secondary research, then we'll address the opportunities and challenges of doing primary research on the Internet. Finally, this chapter will describe some appropriate research for developing a Web presence.

General Strategies for Conducting Research

One of the first things many people tend to think of when they are faced with a need to uncover information is using an Internet search engine. But to conduct effective and rigorous research, we need to develop a research strategy. It therefore pays to think about the topic before plunging into the cold waters of the Internet. There are three key points to consider.

First, Internet research is only one aspect of a well-designed research plan. Many databases, articles, and research sources still are available only in low-tech form, such as books or on-site library-owned CD ROMs. That means that although the Internet can reduce your library time, it can't really supplant it. Sometimes, it's just plain easier to pick up the company phone book than to look up the number on its Web site.

Second, when you use Internet search engines, you should bear in mind that each one is different. They use different methods of collecting data, they store those data differently, and as a result, their databases do not carry identical information. That means if your search comes up empty with one search engine, you cannot assume the information does not exist on the Web. In other words, you should use multiple search engines or a "meta" searching system that works with several engines for your Internet research.

Third, creative research strategies can save you a lot of time. Avoid the trap of falling into a mindset in which you immediately run an Internet search for all the information you need. This is important for three reasons. First, information the Internet is inconsistent and unstable. It is inconsistent in that the quality of the information is sometimes very high, but can also be very poor. The Internet also is unstable because Web sites often are perishable; Web authors move away and leave their sites unattended, sites disappear and leave outdated links on search engines, and servers or ISPs change or expire. Second. search engines do not necessarily prioritize results in a way that will suit your needs. You can save a lot of time you'd otherwise spend sifting irrelevant resources if you can access a direct path to the information you need. Finally, with a little creative thought, you can sometimes target the *best* specific resource for *your* particular question. For example, if you're looking for titles by an author and you know the author has a Web site, you may be better off looking at the Web site than conducting a search through an online library. After all, the author surely is a better authority on his works than the library.

The bottom line is that good research, on or off the Web, incorporates a *combination* of techniques. Go to the library, use electronic databases, try the Web-based search engines, keep an eye on local and world news, and go directly to Web sites you think might offer appropriate information. Include "systematic browsing" in your strategy. Look at the books in the library that are stored on the shelves near those you identify in your catalog searches. On the Web, look at the sites that your searches yield to develop well-targeted keywords for additional searches. Use library databases on CD ROM to find current information on your topic.

Once you have determined that you need to do some searching on the Internet, you're ready to think about which search engine to use. To help you do that, the next section describes various types of engines that you might find on the 'Net.

Techniques for Conducting Internet Searches

The first step in conducting Internet searches is determining which engine or engines best suit your needs. To do that, of course, you need to know something about the nature of those engines and how they differ.

Types of Search Engines

The University of Wisconsin Internet Scout Project[1] has categorized search engines into five general types. Understanding each of those types will help you determine both which combination of searches will suit your needs and which engines are most compatible with your personal research techniques. The first four items on the list are organized roughly in order of increasing precision. The fifth item is a special category.

1. *Searchable Indexes* are simply databases that contain the content of Web pages. Every day, automated "robots" or "spiders" search the Web and install the content of millions of Web sites into these databases. This category also includes "meta-search" engines that allow you to enter in a single process keywords that will be submitted to several different engines.

    Because your search through indexes sifts through some or all of each Web site's content, the results can be overwhelming and poorly focused for your topic. However, they also can yield excellent information, if your search strategy is well defined and targeted. Examples of popular searchable indexes include AltaVista, Excite, HotBot, Infoseek, and Lycos. MetaCrawler is a popular meta-search engine. See the Notes at the end of this chapter for URLs of search engines that have proved to be reasonably stable over time.[2]

2. *Subject Catalogs* provide links to resources that are arranged in categorical hierarchies. Some subject catalogs are searchable, and the search results often indicate the subject under which each Web page is cataloged. Subject catalogs are useful for systematic browsing within broad topics, provided you have a good sense of the category or categories that are appropriate for your topic. Examples of widely used subject catalogs include Yahoo and LookSmart.

3. *Annotated Directories* provide lists of hotlinks to selected Web sites, along with brief summaries of each. Annotated directories are useful for helping you decide whether a page might be useful before you click on the link. Examples of annotated directories include Lycos Top 5% and Magellan.

4. *Subject Guides* are created by subject specialists who first select then annotate each Web site before it is included as a link. These are excellent resources if you are looking for information on a particular subject that is covered by one of these guides. The W3C Virtual Library is an example of a subject guide.

5. *Specialized Directories* offer special tools for Internet resources other than Web sites. These resources allow searches of postings to Usenet newsgroups, information on Web servers, e-mail addresses, and more. Examples of specialized directories include DejaNews, Four11, Switchboard, and Shareware.com.

Each type of search engine offers different information, and each requires a different approach to searching. However, some general guidelines for formulating search strategies can make the task relatively easy.

Developing Keyword Searches

In order to develop techniques that will work for you, it's helpful to know something about how searches are constructed. The University of Wisconsin Internet Scout Project provides a brief overview of the seven search functions that various databases and indexes support. The first six are search techniques with which you should be familiar so you can conduct effective searches: 1) Boolean searching, 2) field searching, 3) keyword in context (KWIC) searching, 4) phrase searching, 5) proximity searching, and 6) truncation searching. The last function concerns the ability of some search engines to give you a sense of the 7) relevance of search results to your particular search.

The next few pages explain the basic concepts of each search function. However, because every search engine is different, you should be sure to read the types of functions that are supported by the particular service you choose to use. Most services provide detailed information on the specific ways in which you should enter your words.

Boolean searching is among the oldest and most widely used of search techniques, and is based on logical mathematical operators. That means it uses terms that will connect your words together in particular ways, such as "and," "or," and "not." For example, suppose you were trying to find information on the effects of television violence on children. You key in the words:

```
television violence
```

Without a Boolean operator, such as "AND" or "NOT," this search will yield all Web pages that include the word "television" *and* all pages that include the word "violence." That means you're likely to get pages that review television sitcoms, pages that report on the Serbian violence against ethnic Albanians, and links to a host of other Web sites that are not related to your topic. The Boolean search allows you to narrow your search by specifying that the page must include both words:

```
television AND violence
```

This search will yield only links to Web sites in which *both* terms appear somewhere in a page. You could narrow the search even further by adding another operator:

```
television AND violence NOT cartoon
```

In this example, the system will yield links only to Web pages that contain both of the terms "television" and "violence," but not the pages that also contain the word "cartoon."

Some systems have a "shortcut" function is similar but not identical to the Boolean "AND." This feature supports the use of a plus sign (+) immediately before a word to indicate that it must be present in the page. Thus, the search for "television" and "violence" would appear:

```
+television +violence
```

Some systems include a Boolean operator as a default connector between words. Be sure to check the search instructions or Frequently Asked Questions (FAQ) files for the particular search engine you're using.

Field searching limits searches to specific areas of a Web page, such as the URL, the title, the headers, the links, the text, the images, and so on. Thus, you can boost the relevance of search results by limiting your search to particular fields. For example, if you know you only want pages that will discuss television violence as a major topic, you might limit the your search to only page headers in which the term "television violence" appears.

Keyword in context (KWIC) searching allows you to define the context in which your search terms appear. You do that by specifying words that should appear near your search terms. For example, in our example of conducting a search on the effects of television violence on children, you might search for "television violence" and include "cartoon" as a contextual keyword.

Phrase searching is particularly useful because it allows you to find a particular phrase, often by delimiting it with quotation marks. Thus, you can find pages that include specific phrases in their entirety. Some systems also support combining phrases with keywords:

```
    "television violence"
or
    cartoons AND "television violence"
```

It's important to pay attention to how or if phrase searching is supported on each system. All too often, people think they're doing a phrase search when the service is really conducting a search for "television OR violence OR cartoons."

Proximity searching also allows you to narrow your search by searching for one word or term that appears within a particular range of another word or term. As an example, you might search for "television violence" that appears within five words of "children."

Truncation searching supports the use of a "wild card" symbol to let you look for various forms of a particular word. For example, if you're interested in what (if anything) television violence *communicates* to children, Web sites that include any form of "communication," "communicative," "communicate," "communicates," "communicated," and so on might be helpful. If the truncation symbol is "*," you can truncate the word as "communic*" so the system will return pages with all forms of it. Of course, you need to give the truncation some careful thought. For example, "commun*" will return words like "communion" and "Communist." Each service describes which, if any, truncation symbols it supports.

In addition to the various searching techniques they support, many search services provide feedback on the relevance of search results. The idea here is to let you know how closely the retrieved pages match your original query. Some *relevance reports* are quantitative, and indicate relevance to your query in terms of 0 to 100 or 0 to 1,000. Others use a system of four or five stars to indicate the highest relevance, on the basis of how well your search term(s) appear on the resulting Web pages.

As you develop your search terms, try to think of words that are *unique* to your topic, and learn which features of your search engines will help you narrow your search. Be sure to keep an eye out for results that can nudge your thinking toward additional descriptive words.

Of course, using search engines is only one way to get information from the Internet. Literally millions of government, corporate, not-for-profit, and educational Web sites that are useful for the public relations practitioner can be directly accessed, as well as hundreds of excellent public relations sites and services.

Discerning the Quality of Information on the Internet

You've found the perfect Web site, chock full of great information! Or have you? Finding the specific information we need in the jumbled mass of Internet resources is only the first of several challenges that we face. A second challenge in using the Web is determining the relative worth of the information we find.

Just about anyone with an html editor and Internet access can slap a Web page onto a server and become a self-proclaimed "expert." This means we need to take extra steps to verify the information we find. Fortunately, the natural and social sciences provide us with some tools that we can adapt for evaluating the quality of information we access through the Internet. In particular, we should consider the general concepts of *validity* and *reliability*.

In broad stroke terms, *validity* refers to the accuracy of the information. In the natural and social sciences, issues of validity concern whether a study measures what it claims to measure. For example, let's say we want to study whether people become generally more active after consuming caffeine. To do that, we measure how many words per minute one group of people talks after drinking two cups of coffee, and compare that to a second group of people who drink two cups of decaffeinated coffee. This study would have very little validity because it doesn't really measure overall *activity*—it measures only verbosity. Furthermore, the study has several other problems that render any data we collect questionable. The point is that several design flaws threaten the validity of study. Similarly, when we look at information on the Internet, we need to be alert for anything that threatens overall legitimacy of the information, including flaws in logic or argument.

Beyond questions of information validity, we should be concerned with issues of *reliability*. Statisticians view reliability in terms of the consistency or stability of the data over time. Clearly both issues are important when we evaluate Web sites and the information they contain. Some sites prove to be both inconsistent and unstable. We know that the Internet, in general, is somewhat unstable as people and servers move to new locations, new users and new technologies connect, host servers become clogged with heavy traffic, and sites expire or become outdated. It's not uncommon for sites to offer valid information, but be unreliable because the server is slow or so congested that it's nearly impossible to access.

Determining Information Validity

Sometimes, validity is reasonably easy to discern. If we want information on the various forms of cancer, for example, the American Cancer Society Web site would be one logical place to start. You know the information is *valid* because the American Cancer Society is a highly credible organization with proven expertise and knowledge in the field of cancer research. However, the validity of information we find on the Internet is not always readily apparent. Therefore, we need to develop some techniques for discerning the extent to which we can depend on various sources and the information they offer.

Jan Alexander and Marsha Tate, reference librarians at Widener University in Pennsylvania, have developed one approach to evaluating the merit of Web pages that is adapted from five traditional

criteria of print media: 1) Accuracy, 2) Authority
3) Objectivity, 4) Currency, and 5) Coverage.

There are no reliable standards for *accuracy* or
honesty on the Web, so you need to verify the content
of Web pages. First, try to determine whether the
source of the information uses fact checkers. If you're
reading the online version of the *Los Angeles Times*,
you know some journalistic fact checking was
involved. But if you're looking at a high school
student's personal Web site, you should be very
cautious as to whether the facts presented were
checked for accuracy. That puts the burden of double
checking the information on you, and means you'll
need to find other resources to verify the material. It
also brings us to the idea of *authority*.

If you're considering a Web site as a source of
information, you need to take into account the
qualifications of the site owner. Is this person or
organization a bona fide expert or *authority* on the
subject? What qualifications does the author have to
present the information, and how credible is the
publisher of the site? All too often, it is difficult to tell
who the author was, what their qualifications might
be, and the extent to which the publisher of the site
assumes responsibility for its content. For example,
Web sites at educational institutions often are difficult
to verify. It is not immediately clear if you are
reading a Web page created by a faculty member or
by a student, nor is it always apparent if the site
represents an official university-sponsored program,
or if it merely espouses one individual's personal
agenda.

If the site is promoting any particular agenda or agendas, it is not objective. *Objectivity* refers to the extent to which the source of the Web site is free from bias. Look for puff words, overstated generalities, and other propagandistic or manipulative techniques, particularly if the purpose of the site is not clearly stated. If the site appears biased, the information on it will require careful cross checking. Most commercial Web sites, for example, are presenting material that favors the organizations they represent. This means the Web sites are authoritative on the products and services they describe, but also may contain information that is biased in favor of those products and services.

Currency refers to how up-to-date information that appears on a Web site might be. Look for dates of creation and/or revision on every page of a Web site. If only the front page indicates a revision date, you cannot assume that every page received similar attention on the same day. Unless you visit a site regularly, you also may not be able to discern if a date refers to the date of creation or the date of the last revision. If the date is not recent, the information may be outdated or obsolete.

Finally, check the depth and breadth of the material that the Web site presents. Does the content *coverage* appear comprehensive? Does it offer supporting evidence for its content, or does it simply make sweeping statements without appropriate research, statistics, examples, and the like?

By using these five criteria as the basis for your evaluation, you can develop some sense of the validity of the Web site and whether its content is usable as the basis for your campaign or program. However, you also want to consider the reliability of the site, especially if you expect the material to play an important role in your planning.

Determining Information Reliability

Several factors are involved in determining the reliability of a Web site. Here, you want to consider the relative stability of the Web site over time, and try to identify some indicators of that stability. Some characteristics to look for include 1) a unique domain name, 2) a stable Web site publisher, 3) the quality of the Web site design and organization, and 4) accessibility of the site.

Turning again to our example of the American Cancer Society national Web site, you can see that it probably is reasonably reliable for several reasons. First, the domain name is registered to the American Cancer Society (cancer.org). As mentioned in Chapter 1, this means that even if the ACS moves its offices, you'll probably be able to find the Web site at the same URL. Second, the national organization is stable and widely recognized. You probably can assume it will be around for a while. Third, the site is well designed and well organized. It clearly exhibits care and planning. Fourth, the site and its links all are accessible and operate well. The server is not congested by more traffic than it can handle, and the connection seems stable.

So far, we've focused on Web pages, searching systems, and online libraries as sources of information, but the Internet allows information

gathering in other ways to support public relations
activities. In fact, online qualitative and quantitative
primary research is changing the face of public
relations.

Advantages & Challenges of Internet Research

Beyond storing information for and about a client's
interests, the Internet presents both opportunities and
challenges for conducting primary research. As we
saw in Chapter 3, new online publics emerge as
global entities through Listservs, newsgroups, chat
rooms, and other Internet-based services. Clearly, it is
important to gather information from and about
online New Publics. Both qualitative and quantitative
data are available through a variety of online research
techniques.

Qualitative Research Methods

Qualitative research involves information that
addresses human experiences in ways that cannot
necessarily be measured with numbers. Public
relations practitioners have a long history of gathering
qualitative data through such techniques as focus
groups, informal interviews, and ethnographic
methods. A number of these techniques translate very
nicely to the world of cyberspace.

As we saw in Chapter 3, it is important to recognize
and establish communication with the New Publics
that emerge online. Identifying and participating in

virtual communities can provide new opportunities for environmental scanning, surveillance, competitive intelligence, and issues tracking. This means it's important to stay abreast of newly developing groups, and to participate in them on a regular basis.

The purpose of monitoring newsgroups and other online communities is threefold, and spans several steps of the four-step process. First, it enables the practitioner to monitor candid conversations that concern the client. Second, it provides client representation for two-way communication with target publics. Third, it provides client services to target publics, such as customer services for consumers.

Research advantages of "hanging out" in online communities include the ability to gather rich qualitative data, the identification of potential opinion leaders, and early detection of developing issues. The major disadvantage of monitoring and participating in online communities is that it's labor intensive, which means it can be fairly expensive, both in terms of money and in terms of time.

Online "interviews" also generate useful qualitative data. The information may be gathered in combination with formal quantitative survey instruments, which are described in the next section, or online qualitative questionnaires can be used as stand-alone tools. In both cases, the information is gathered through questions that computer users answer through Web-based "forms" or through e-mail. The answers to the questions then are transmitted automatically to the client for analysis and interpretation.

Another technique that utilizes qualitative data is the online focus group. Here, both nonsimultaneous forms of CMC, such as Listservs or similar e-mail distribution lists, and simultaneous forms, such as chat rooms, can serve as low-cost venues for gathering qualitative information. In online focus groups, voluntary participants answer and discuss a series of questions. Similar to a face-to-face focus group, this technique allows the practitioner to gather rich information about representative groups' feelings, ideas, and opinions. The advantages include:

➤ Cost reductions in comparison to traditional face-to-face focus groups, because travel and transportation are not necessary.
➤ Convenience for participants in nonsimultaneous venues, because they can log in as they choose to discuss and respond to questions.
➤ Automatic word-for-word transcriptions of online conversations and responses to questions.

In addition to online monitoring and environmental scanning, many clients are utilizing online quantitative research methods.

Quantitative Research Methods

Quantitative research entails the gathering and analysis of data that can be measured with numbers. Counting the frequency of how many people access a Web site or measuring an opinion on a scale of one to ten with ten being best are simple examples of quantitative data.

The online marketing and public relations survey is rapidly becoming a bedrock tool of public relations and marketing. Thousands of Web sites now offer incentives for visitors to participate in information exchange with client organizations. This research technique not only provides information to the client, but it also can engage the Web user in the client's Web site.

The following list illustrates some research advantages of Web-based surveys:

➢ Gathering and preparing the data for analysis with automated programs is relatively easy through simple automated programs.
➢ The method of data gathering is non-intrusive. Participants voluntarily respond while they are logged on to the Web site.
➢ An international audience can be reached because the Internet is a global medium.
➢ Costs of data gathering and analysis can be relatively low because the technology enables automated functions.
➢ Participants can receive an immediate response that thanks them for taking part in the survey.
➢ Participants can receive immediate incentives for participating, such as enrollment in a random drawing or a free screen saver.
➢ Data can be transferred immediately to a database, for speedy analysis and reporting.

Of course, Web-based research techniques also have limitations that can threaten the validity and reliability of the research. The following issues can result in potential problems for Web-based research:

> ➤ Technological limitations can render accurate response rates difficult to determine.
> ➤ Internet-based questionnaires often have low response rates in comparison to traditional paper-and-pencil surveys.
> ➤ Similar to traditional surveys, respondents are self-selected, which may result in biased data.
> ➤ Respondents access Web-based surveys only if they have a particular interest in the client, either because they are experiencing some sort of difficulty and are seeking a remedy on the Web site (potential negative bias), or because they are enthusiastic about the client's product or service (potential positive bias). Sometimes, of course, you want a biased sample. For example, if you want to identify and rectify problems that may exist in customer relations, data drawn from the responses of dissatisfied customers may uncover meaningful patterns or trends.
> ➤ Only respondents with Internet access can participate, which may limit the sample to a particular demographic and psychographic profile.
> ➤ Survey instruments must be prepared in multiple languages, if multinational responses are desired.

Structuration tells us that CMC is both the medium and the outcome of its interactions and processes. This idea implies that the Internet can serve as both a tool and a reason for conducting research. In other words, before developing a Web presence, research similar to that done before implementing any public relations tool is necessary. Too often, this idea is overlooked, in the enthusiasm of developing a "cool" new Web site.

What You Need to Know before You Develop Your Client's Web Presence

"Build it and they will come." In the movie *Field of Dreams*, Kevin Costner built a baseball diamond at the direction of those words. Today, people build Web sites based on pretty much the same rationale. Certainly, Web sites have become important public relations tools, particularly when integrated into a multipronged campaign, but it's important to develop them as systematically as any other communication program—and that means following the same four-step process. As a result, you'll need to do some research to determine the client's goals and objectives, the resources available for Web site construction and maintenance, and the technologies that are appropriate for the type of Web site that will best suit the client's needs.

First, you'll need to determine the purpose a Web site will serve. What organizational or public relations goals will it help you meet? What does the client really want to accomplish? If the Web site is part of a multidimensional campaign, the answers to those questions may be readily apparent. But if you just got a call from out of the blue, and the client is requesting a Web site, you may need to elicit the answers. That means you'll need to do the same sort of diagnostic work you would do any time a client jumps into tools before clearly defining the public relations problem. You'll need to determine exactly what the problem is, what the goal is, who the target publics are, and what the client hopes to gain.

Second, the planning of a Web site demands a number of technical considerations that other public relations tools do not. One major problem that any technological innovation tends to create is a bottleneck at the technical level. Here, you need to find out if the client has a plan for Web maintenance as well as development. This can be a costly and time-consuming aspect of the Web site, if it requires frequent updating or if it is particularly large.

Third, well-designed Web sites incorporate two-way communication between the client and visitors to the site. This means the client must have the resources to respond efficiently and effectively to a potentially large volume of e-mail inquiries. All too often, clients find themselves bombarded with more e-mail than they possibly can handle. If the client cannot respond to e-mail quickly, the Web site will do more public relations harm than good.

Fourth, the client needs to plan for demands that will be placed on the host server. If high volume traffic is expected, a high-speed, multi-processor server may be necessary. Maintenance of the hardware also is a serious consideration. If the client expects to use the Web site to reduce the telephone burden of customer service, some capability of 24-hour maintenance will be required.

Fifth, determine what sorts of technological resources will be necessary for Web site development. Multimedia Web sites can be major investments, in terms of design expertise, special software applications, and programming and debugging.

Finally, it's a good idea to research the possibility of registering a domain name to enhance the client's name recognition. Research here will involve finding out what names are available and what similar names might be in use or come into use that could have embarrassing ramifications to your client (such as pornographic sites with very similar domain names). Consider the possibility of registering several permutations of a domain name to maintain control of the client's name.

Chapter Summary

The Internet can help us do primary research in which we collect, analyze, and report the data, as well as secondary research in which we gather information that has been archived by others. Search engines are helpful for doing secondary research on the Internet, but their use should be combined with other research techniques, both on- and off-line. Five general types of search engines are 1) searchable indexes, 2) subject catalogs, 3) annotated directories, 4) subject guides, and 5) specialized directories. Search techniques that various systems support include 1) Boolean searching, 2) field searching, 3) keyword in context (KWIC) searching, 4) phrase searching, 5) proximity searching, and 6) truncation searching. In addition, some systems offer feedback on the 7) relevance of search results for your particular search.

Public relations practitioners can use a variety of techniques to determine the quality of resources on the Internet, and whether it is useful as part of their research. Issues of validity and reliability concern overall quality of information. One technique for

determining validity adapts five traditional criteria for
print: 1) Accuracy, 2) Authority 3) Objectivity,
4) Currency, and 5) Coverage. Issues of reliability
concern the general stability and accessibility of the
Web site.

Internet research offers a variety of advantages and
disadvantages to the public relations practitioner.
General advantages include speed, interactivity with
target publics, early identification of opinion leaders,
the ability to reach multinational audiences, and cost
reductions. Disadvantages can include bias of sample
and data, low response rates, and technological
limitations. Because Web users are both self-selected
and representative of only a portion of the population,
online survey techniques should be used only as part
of an information-gathering program.

Considerable research is necessary for the
development of a Web site. Key considerations
include: 1) the client's goals and objectives, 2) the
client's ability to maintain the site, 3) the client's
ability to respond to e-mail that the site yields,
4) projected demands on the host server,
5) technological resources required for Web site
development, and 6) a recognizable and unique
domain name to enhance the client's identity
recognition.

Exercises

1. Find a synopsis of the Herman Melville novel *Moby Dick* through the following search engines:

   a) AltaVista
   b) Yahoo
   c) Lycos
   d) MetaCrawler

   Which engine did you find easiest to use? Which did you find most difficult? Why? Which types of searches (e.g., Boolean, keyword in context) does each system support?

2. Locate five large corporate Web sites of your choice. Do the domain names reflect the corporate identity? Can you determine if the corporation is gathering quantitative information? Is there evidence of an online survey or other Web-based data-gathering tool? Are qualitative data being gathered? Reflect on the types of online research described in this chapter, and see if you can identify them on the sites you visit.

3. How would you rate the quality of the information on each of the five sites you found for #2 above, in terms of accuracy, authority objectivity, currency, and coverage? Do you consider the sites reliable? Why or why not?

References

Alexander, J., & Tate, M. A. (1999). *Evaluating Web resources*. Available:
http://www.science.widener.edu/~withers/webeval.htm

Internet Scout Project. (1998). Searching the Internet. *Internet Scout Toolkit* University of Wisconsin. Available:
http://wwwscout.cs.wisc.edu/scout/toolkit/searching/index.html

Smith, M. J. (1988). *Contemporary communication research methods*. Belmont, CA: Wadsworth.

Notes

[1] Internet Scout Project. (1998). *Internet Scout Toolkit. [On-Line]*. University of Wisconsin. Available: http://wwwscout.cs.wisc.edu/scout/toolkit/index.html

[2] Although most of this book avoids including URLs, which tend to be dated before printed materials can be produced, the following search engines are widely used, and have proved stable for some time:

- AltaVista— http://altavista.digital.com/
- Deja News— http://www.dejanews.com/
- Excite— http://www.excite.com/
- Four11— http://www.four11.com/
- HotBot— http://www.hotbot.com/
- Infoseek— http://www.infoseek.com/
- LookSmart— http://www.looksmart.com/
- Lycos— http://www.lycos.com/
- Lycos Top 5%— http://point.lycos.com/categories/
- Magellan— http://www.mckinley.com/
- MetaCrawler— http://www.metacrawler.com/
- Shareware.com— http://www.shareware.com/
- Switchboard— http://www.switchboard.com/
- The W3C Virtual Library— http://www.w3c.org/vl/
- Yahoo— http://www.yahoo.com/

Chapter 5. Planning

The Second Step

Learning Objectives

This chapter addresses the second step of the four-step public relations process, planning. While planning is a crucial step in effective public relations, it also is the one for which the Internet offers the fewest resources. However, the electronic environment does provide some useful tools for this phase of the public relations process. Key topics covered in this chapter include:

➢ Management by objectives for public relations.
➢ Writing effective objectives.
➢ Internet resources for PR-MBO.
➢ Planning the development of a Web presence.

Planning for Public Relations

We all make plans. We plan our retirements, we plan
our vacations, we plan for parties—our worlds are
filled with plans. The more systematically we develop
our plans, the better prepared we are to save enough
money for a comfortable retirement, get the best rates
on vacation travel, and graciously host our guests.
Planning for public relations is no different. This
chapter describes some specific techniques to plan a
public relations campaign or program that will enable
you to determine your progress toward attaining your
public relations goals as well as assist you in
evaluating the overall effectiveness of your public
relations undertaking. One way to do that is through
management by objectives (MBO), which was first
developed by Professor Peter F. Drucker on the basis
of his research, then fully described in the early '60s
by George S. Odiorne. Used in a variety of contexts
and under a variety of names, MBO became very
popular as a management tool in the '80s, and
remains in wide use today in numerous forms.

MBO originally was developed as a way to involve
employees in the managerial capacity of establishing
accountability and measurability. Norman Nager of
Cal State Fullerton and T. Harrell Allen of East
Carolina University have applied it to the practice of
public relations as a management function, which
they call Public Relations-Management by Objectives
(PR-MBO).

PR-MBO not only provides accountability and
measurability, but it enables the practitioner to
determine if a project is on course while it is

underway. Like many aerospace, engineering, and military organizations, we can think of MBO as similar to the flight plan a pilot files before taking off from the airport. The plan outlines the route the pilot will take, the estimated times that the aircraft will pass over certain landmarks, and an estimated time of arrival. It tells both the pilot and the air traffic controllers if the plane is on course, if its progress is proceeding as expected, and if it will reach its destination as planned. If the pilot runs into a storm, the route can be modified to avoid it, and the flight plan can be modified. Then, once the plane has reached its destination, the pilot can assess if the trip were successful, in terms of:

➢ travel quality for passengers (did they experience a lot of turbulence?),
➢ timeliness (did the aircraft land on time?),
➢ use of resources (was fuel consumption more or less than expected?), and
➢ outcome (was the flight diverted to an alternate destination?).

MBO is much the same for us in public relations as the flight plan is for the pilot. We literally write a plan that outlines the ultimate destination for our campaign (the goal), lay out each landmark along the way (the objectives), and establish measurement techniques to help us determine our progress. When objectives are well conceived and well written, they provide target dates, budgetary guidelines, and other indicators of both how a public relations project is progressing while it is in progress, and how well it was accomplished after it is completed.

Writing Objectives for Public Relations

Objectives are truly useful only when they're carefully written. Therefore, it's a good idea to review here some basic techniques for writing effective public relations goals and objectives. As we learned in Chapter 2, goals are general directions for action, and they express our aspirations for the future. For example, your public relations goal might be to improve the name recognition of your client for the general public. Objectives, on the other hand, are very specific, and help measure your progress toward attainment of your stated goal. Therefore, an example of an objective to support our goal of improved name recognition might be to write and administer a benchmark survey that asks about the client's name recognition to 500 people in the community by December 31.

Writing clear, meaningful objectives takes practice and thought. The first step in PR-MBO is to establish the goal or goals you want to accomplish. Then, you can write the objectives that will help you reach the goal. Nager and Allen point out that asking yourself *why* and *how* can help you determine your goals and objectives. The *why* is the goal; the *how* is the objective. In other words, you ask yourself *why* you want to launch your public relations campaign, then develop the specifics for *how* you will do it. Of course, this isn't always a simple task, so a schematic "tree" like the one depicted in Figure 5.1 can be a helpful aid.

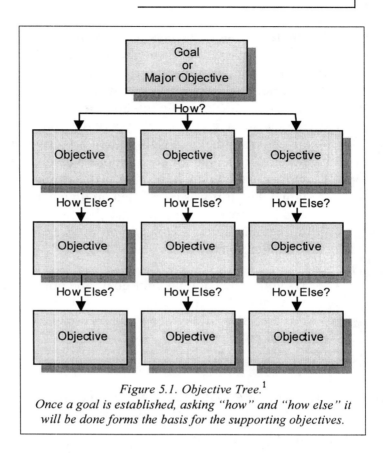

Figure 5.1. Objective Tree.[1]
Once a goal is established, asking "how" and "how else" it will be done forms the basis for the supporting objectives.

Similarly, if you have some objectives in mind, and you "have a feeling" they're on the right track but you can't quite voice your goal, try reversing the process by asking *why*. The answer should state what you ultimately want to accomplish—in other words, your goal.

When writing your objectives, if you take care to include three key characteristics, you'll find they will help you create your budgets, timelines, and other modes of campaign evaluation. Each objective should be 1) specific, 2) measurable, and 3) bound by time. This means your objective should only address a single, well-focused task that *directly relates* to the accomplishment of the goal. It also should be measurable, in terms of quantity, quality, or costs. Chapter 7 addresses measurement techniques that are used to evaluate public relations activities, so you may want to read it to help you write your own objectives. Finally, a well-written objective should have a target date for completion. If an objective is written well, you will be able to determine on the target date if it was completed on time, within budget, and in a manner that meets the client's needs. Most important, you will know if you're on course for attaining your goal.

As you're developing your goals and objectives, you inevitably need little bits of information. As in the research step of the four-step process, the Internet can be helpful here.

Internet Resources for PR-MBO

As you're putting together your timelines and budgets, you're likely to be projecting some time into the future. The Internet offers a wealth of resources for comparison pricing to establish budget items, calendars to help with timelines, and extensive travel-related information. Beyond that, e-mail provides a fast and cost-efficient way to collaborate on design and planning with colleagues and clients. Full design layouts can be exchanged via e-mail attachments, ftp, and the Web. In addition, computer conferencing, Listservs, and other electronic discussion lists can be invaluable tools.

Numerous public relations-specific Web sites exist
that provide useful tools for segmenting target
publics, listing online journalistic outlets, and the like.
But one often-overlooked resource is the "electronic
water cooler,"[2] where public relations professionals
gather to exchange ideas, seek advice on problems,
and brainstorm. Some of these venues are
conversational and social; others are unrelentingly
formal and professional. All of them, however, offer
valuable resources for the professional.

Topics of conversation in e-mail distribution lists
sometimes seem trivial at first glance, but become an
important part of the planning process. For example,
the topic of nametags arose several years ago on one
list. Someone posted a message that clip-on nametags
at an event had garnered a complaint as being sexist
because women often didn't have lapels or pockets
that would accommodate them. Some discussion
followed concerning the types of nametags that were
most suitable for large gatherings. Adhesive-backed
tags were problematic on silk garments, clips didn't
work well without pockets or lapels, and pins
damaged some fabrics. One viable solution was the
neck strap badge, which could be worn comfortably
and did not require any special features in clothing.

No matter what your feeling about the relative merits
of the nametag problem, in terms of sexism or
significance, these sorts of issues arise every day in
the world of public relations. Because we know
perception is important, it pays to be prepared and to
plan for as many of these sorts of problems as we
possibly can. The e-mail exchange may have averted
other similar problems for practitioners who read the
thread and made a note of alternative solutions for

nametags at events. This conversation illustrates the value of interacting, both online and off, with fellow practitioners. The Internet is one way to do it without having to interrupt a project or travel across town.

We've seen some general types of planning resources the Internet provides. It also represents part of a campaign that requires planning.

Planning the Development of a Web Presence

Planning a Web presence does not need to be exceptionally complex, but it does require some thought. In the first, research step of the four-step process, resources and technological requirements were established and you elicited some basic information from the client. In this second step, you'll establish clear goals and objectives for the Web site. Write down your goal: *Why* are you developing this Web site? Examples: To provide consumer service; to enhance a unique corporate identity; to deliver news to the media. Then write down the objectives: *How* will you accomplish this goal? By when? Measured in what way? Example: Develop a questionnaire to develop a consumer profile for incorporation into the Web site by May 1.

You may decide that a major goal of the Web site is to gather information from target publics, as well as deliver information to them. That means you need to incorporate into your plan the level of sophistication (and expense) the data gathering on the Web site will require. If you need sophisticated surveillance and recording of information, your investment will be larger. A simple Web-based questionnaire and a counter of "hits" to the site, on the other hand, will be relatively inexpensive.

Plan the content to match targeted audiences, goals, and the Internet community. You might need to draw on focus group research for this stage of the planning. Also consider the criteria for high-quality content that we borrowed from print media. Design your content with the concepts of accuracy, authority, objectivity, currency, and coverage (as described in Chapter 4) in mind.

It's a good idea to establish a timeline for development. This means setting dates for benchmark tasks, such as purchasing or outsourcing the host computer, hiring designers and programmers, acquiring any special software required, developing the overall look, determining multimedia capabilities and requirements, creating a site map, and so forth. Most of these dates can be drawn directly from your objectives. Example objectives might be:

1. Hire photographer by July 1.
2. Take product photos by July 20.
3. Determine software needs by July 15.
4. Purchase software by August 1.

With these objectives in mind, your partial timeline might look something like the example in Table 5.1.

TASK	July				August			
	1	15	20	25	1	15	20	25
1. Hire Photographer	X							
2. Photos Shot			X					
3. Determine Software		X						
4. Purchase Software					X			

Table 5.1. Sample Timeline Drawn from Objectives.

Thinking Ahead

One of the key aspects of planning a Web site is determining how it will be used and developing a site map. This means figuring out what components you want to include, which audiences will access each of the components, and determining how you want them to be connected. Is the primary goal for the Web site consumer relations and customer service? Is it financial and investor relations? Will it gather marketing information from visitors? Perhaps it will do all of those things and more. In any event, you'll need to plan what types of information you want to transmit and to receive for each target public and for each type of activity the site is intended to support.

In addition to content and style of the site, plan for its future support. Will you want to sell advertising space and offer banner ads? Consider the possibility of targeting specific types of ads to specific content pages. You'll also need to establish advertising rates and specifications for ads you will accept.

At this stage, it's a good idea to draw actual diagrams or flow charts of the site that depicts how the pages will link and how the files on the server will be organized. Figure 5.2 illustrates a simple diagram of a Web site. Obviously, this step requires some

understanding of what constitutes good Web design
and structure, which will be covered in Chapter 6 of
this handbook. Perhaps you want to replicate all or
part of a magazine or other printed materials. That
may mean creating a storyboard for the site. The key,
here, is to think ahead and to plan for expansion.

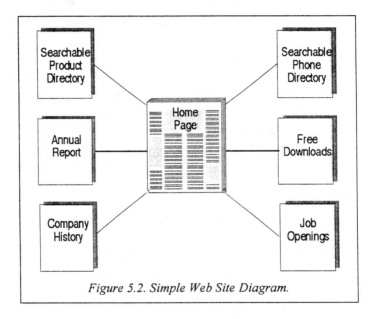

Figure 5.2. Simple Web Site Diagram.

Anticipating Change

Small things overlooked at this stage can become
technical and maintenance nightmares. For example,
if you think you may eventually want a full annual
report online, organize your file directories to
accommodate it now, even if this year, you'll simply
post a single-page, text-only profit-and-loss
statement. Create separate directories for images, so
you won't have image documents cluttering up the
server. The better you plan the site and the server

directories at this point, the easier it will be to update, modify, and expand in the future.

One crucial aspect of the planning process is the recognition that the Web is, at this point, a largely uncontrolled medium. That means that no matter how carefully you have constructed your Web site, no matter how lovingly you have selected your fonts, no matter how painstakingly you have developed your color schemes, you have little or no control over how the visitor to your site will actually view it. If layout and format is critical to your message, consider using .pdf files, which maintain all formatting and are viewed through a free program by Adobe called Acrobat Reader. This technique is particularly useful if you want a manual or report to appear on the screen precisely as it does in print form.

Considering the Web as an uncontrolled medium affects your site planning. Most Web designers recognize that the average modem user still has a 15" screen, a 56K modem, and monitor resolution of 832 X 624. But some people are still using much lower resolutions, others are on even slower modems, and still others configure their browsers to override your font sizes, styles, and colors. This means that your planning should include alternatives for people who cannot or will not view your site under optimal circumstances.

Give some thought at this early stage, too, to how people might actually use your site. If they're simply accessing it to play games or to download files, that racy black screen with gold-tone stripe may be just fine. But if you expect your site to be text-intensive and the content is something people will want to print

out on their personal printers, you'll want to keep the
background very light and the text very dark for ease
of reading and efficient printing.

Finally, as with any public relations plan, keep your
target publics in mind. The nature of your client, the
nature of the target audiences, and the overall culture
of the Internet all affect the ways in which you'll
develop your Web site.

Chapter Summary

Effective public relations depends on effective
planning. Public relations management by objectives
establishes specific, time bound, and quantifiable
objectives to support each goal. Goals are established
by asking *why* the project is being undertaken.
Objectives are established by asking *how* the goal will
be accomplished.

The Internet offers a variety of resources for
planning, including e-mail collaboration, computer
conferencing, and electronic discussion lists. The
informal conversations of some discussion lists can
provide opportunities to exchange ideas and
brainstorm on a casual basis.

Planning a Web presence requires establishing clear
goals for doing so. Therefore, the practitioner must
establish the main purpose the Web site is intended to
serve, then develop the objectives that will help attain
the goal. Planning ahead and for the uncontrolled
nature of the ways people view Web sites is
particularly important for the development of an
effective Web presence.

Exercises

1. Write down one personal goal that you would like to attain in the next year or two. Write down three supporting objectives. Make sure each objective explains *how* you will accomplish the goal and that the goal explains *why* you would complete the objective. Don't forget that each objective must be measurable, must be bound by time (have a single target date), and must be measurable.

2. Visit at least five corporate and not-for-profit Web sites. Can you discern what public relations goals they are designed to accomplish?

3. Reflect on the use of e-mail and electronic discussion lists for collaboration and planning. Do you think this is a useful tool? Why or why not? Justify your answer.

References

Drucker, P. F. (1964). *Managing for results; economic tasks and risk-taking decisions*. (1st ed.). New York, Harper & Row.

Gaffin, A., & Heitkötter, J. *Big dummy's guide to the Internet*. Available: http://medisg.stanford.edu/hypertext/net/dummy_guide/bdgtti-1.02_toc.html

Grunig, J. E. & Hunt, T. T (1984). *Managing public relations*. New York: Holt, Rinehart & Winston.

Kendall, R. (1996). *Public relations campaign strategies*. New York: HarperCollins.

Nager, N. R., & Allen, T. H. (1984). *Public relations: Management by objectives*. New York: Longman.

Odiorne, G. S. (1961). *How managers make things happen*. Englewood Cliffs, NJ: Prentice-Hall.

Odiorne, G. S. (1965) *Management by objectives: a system of managerial leadership*. New York: Pitman.

Wilcox, D. L., Ault, P. H., & Agee, W. K. (1998). *Public relations: Strategies and tactics*. New York: Addison Wesley Longman.

Notes

[1] Figure adapted from Nager, N. R., & Allen, T. H. (1984). *Public relations: Management by objectives.* New York: Lanham, MD: University Press, p. 76.

[2] Howard Reingold is one of the several leaders in the field to have likened online discussions to "electronic water coolers." See, for example, Reingold, H. (1993) "A slice of life in my virtual community." In A. Gaffin & J. Heitkötter. *Big dummy's guide to the Internet.* Available: http://medisg.stanford.edu/hypertext/net/dummy_guide/bdgtti-1.02_toc.html

Chapter 6. Execution

The Third Step

Learning Objectives

This chapter describes the third step of the public relations process, execution, in which the practitioner develops and uses specific public relations tools for a campaign or program. This chapter describes ways in which the Internet is used for specific public relations functions, and offers some general guidelines for online public relations. Major topics covered in the next few pages include:

➤ General "netiquette" for simultaneous and nonsimultaneous CMC.
➤ Internet uses for specific public relations functions.
➤ Basic techniques for online public relations.
➤ Tools for authoring and launching a Web site.

Discovering New Capabilities through the 'Net

The Internet is changing the face of public relations, because it both offers new, speedy ways to reach traditional media gatekeepers and new ways to bypass them for direct communication with target publics. At the same time, public relations practices are changing the nature of the Internet as corporate, governmental, not-for-profit, and financial organizations launch Web sites to meet public relations goals. In a structuration sense, then, the Internet and the field of public relations are reciprocally changing each other, and the trend promises to continue.

Web sites now provide news releases in electronic form for journalists, editors, and casual passersby. Direct marketing and e-commerce are booming. Click-through banner advertisements help subsidize many informational Web sites. Businesses are augmenting their customer services and support through the Web and e-mail. Virtual Reality Markup Language (VRML) allows car shoppers to explore panoramic views of automobile interiors. In short, the increasingly sophisticated capabilities of the Web offer public relations opportunities that are hampered only by the practitioner's imagination. This chapter provides a few "starter" ideas for using the Internet in a variety of public relations efforts. Chapter 8 will also address some specialized applications and cases. First, we should consider some basic tips on using computer-mediated communication.

Ten Tips for Practicing Good Netiquette

Because this chapter addresses a variety of ways in which you might use both simultaneous and nonsimultaneous forms of communication, it would not be complete without some general hints on using good "netiquette." Violating the norms, expectations, and values (structures of legitimation and signification) of Internet users can result in a significant loss of credibility for the practitioner. It's therefore critical for the novice user to become familiar with at least some basic rules of netiquette. The following ten tips for might be considered a basic set upon which you can build.

1. Read any FAQs, overviews, introductions, or other information that will help you get oriented to the articulated rules and norms that govern an online group, both simultaneous (such as a chat room) and nonsimultaneous (such as a newsgroup or Listserv).

2. Be sure to "lurk" (read without posting to public discussions) for a while whenever you join a new Usenet newsgroup or e-mail discussion list. Get a feel for the unspoken rules and norms that govern the group.

3. Use appropriate "Internet style" when composing e-mail messages. Avoid typing in all capital letters, because CAPS ARE THE INTERNET EQUIVALENT OF SHOUTING. Avoid heavy ASCII art in your signature line. If you use an "autosignature," limit the line count to four lines

or so, to minimize wasted bandwidth and scrolling for the recipient.

4. *Never* send unsolicited mass e-mailings to discussion list or newsgroup members. This is called *spamming*, and can result in your being losing your ISP, and maybe even losing your client.

5. Do include a signature that identifies you and your institutional affiliation in a manner appropriate for each online group. Some groups consider the inclusion of degrees and titles pretentious; others consider them an important form of self-identification.

6. Avoid dense, lengthy messages. People tend to use their delete buttons rather than expend much energy in reading a lot of text online. Similarly, take a conservative approach in attaching files to your e-mail messages. Many people do not open e-mail attachments, often for fear of an invasion of computer viruses.

7. Avoid quoting entire messages when using an e-mail reply feature. Edit out the sections to which you are not directly responding. When replying to a message from an e-mail discussion list, delete the entire thing if at all possible, in consideration of individuals who get their messages in "digest" form. Digests combine all the e-mail that was sent to a list during a specified time period, so quoted replies result in multiple copies of the same original note appearing in a single message.

8. Save and refer to introductory information from e-mail discussion lists on posting, server commands, and procedures for signing off. Take care to send server commands to the server rather than to the list.

9. Although spelling and grammar often don't count in e-mail, they *both* count in e-mail to professional groups or individuals. Many e-mail programs now include spell checkers. If yours doesn't, try composing your message in a good word processor, then copying-and-pasting it into the body of your e-mail message.

10. Forward information judiciously, and avoid spreading rumors, hoaxes, and urban legends, which abound on the Internet. A number of excellent Web sites provide up-to-date information on urban legends, chain letters, and other forms of Internet hoaxes. Bookmark a couple and use them to check out any announcements that come your way, including those from otherwise reliable sources—especially if the announcements are warnings about a product or organization.

Media Relations on the Internet

Public relations practitioners are significant news resources for media, and many newspapers have online editions that replicate in whole or in part their hardcopy editions. As a result, we're seeing increasing numbers of media representatives who are utilizing the Internet to gather news. PR practitioners can access readymade lists of journalists and editors who accept electronic news releases, and should augment them to develop localized media lists. Electronic news releases save time and energy for everyone, both because of the transmission speed and because the material in electronic form is ready for editing and typesetting without a need for re-entry into a media outlet's computer system.

Of course, not all newspapers or journalists can or will accept electronic news releases. Some prefer faxes, and some prefer snail mail or hand delivery. In this, as in all media relations, it is crucial for the practitioner to develop a personal relationship with each of the media representatives, and to send all materials in the format each recipient prefers. In other words, bedrock methods like introducing oneself to editors, maintaining up-to-date media lists, sensitivity to publication deadlines, and maintaining careful files of specific editorial policies for each outlet remain as important as ever for the practitioner.

The Internet can help you establish media relations through nonsimultaneous discussion groups, such as Usenet newsgroups and Listservs. A number of such discussion groups exist on the Internet, and they offer public relations practitioners excellent opportunities to meet journalists, observe discussions about the field of journalism, and learn journalistic preferences for various media. It's not necessary to participate actively. "Lurking" can provide you with a wealth of information. Two excellent starting points for identifying and joining e-mail discussion groups are the Tile.net and Onelist Web sites. Both services offer extensive listings of online discussion groups, descriptions of the interests around which the groups center, and user-friendly instructions for subscribing to the list. The URLs are:

```
http://www.tile.net/
http://www.onelist.net/
```

One phenomenon that practitioners should be aware of and try to avoid is what we might call the "inquiry article." The ease of adding e-mail attachments tempts some practitioners to ask editors if they are interested in story ideas by sending full-blown releases or feature articles along with the inquiry. This practice may seem like a convenient method of giving the editor the benefit of all your information for consideration, but is more likely to result in it being deleted from the file. A better alternative is to send a traditional pitch letter in advance of the article or story, and then use appropriate e-mail or telephone follow-up.

Media relations through the Internet are becoming routine modes of communication for practitioners and media representatives, but the electronic environment offers opportunities for nearly every other aspect of public relations, as well. In addition to media relations, practitioners can exploit the features of the Internet for a variety of public relations functions, including consumer relations, issues tracking, crisis communication, marketing communications, government affairs, employment opportunities, and investor relations.

Consumer Relations & Marketing on the Internet

One cornerstone public relations opportunity on the Internet resides in using the Web for consumer relations. Web sites can provide current and potential customers information about products, services, pricing, and specifications. As a communication medium, the Web directly reaches geographically expansive target markets without having to pass through traditional media gatekeepers. In addition, the Web offers excellent opportunities for customer care, online payment centers and billing inquiries, and late-breaking news like product updates, newly expanded services, or product recalls.

As we saw in Chapter 3, the emergence of new online publics is making it necessary for us to rethink the ways in which we segment and target the people we hope to reach. One way to do this is through issues tracking and surveillance by participating in appropriate chat rooms, Usenet newsgroups, and e-mail discussion groups. A recognizable spokesperson in these venues can go far toward strengthening of consumer relations, early detection of emergent issues or consumer concerns, and quick response to customer complaints and queries.

Beyond newsgroups and e-mail discussions, the Web offers a number of tools for consumer relations and marketing. Cookie technology, as described in Chapter 3, is one such tool. Newspapers and product vendors have been using cookies for some time to enable users to tailor the ways in which they view Web sites. This means that as New Publics emerge, messages can be prepared and delivered directly to them. For example, interactive forms allow consumers to create and price products built to meet unique specifications. Information submitted on forms also can be used to identify and target emerging New Publics.

In addition to cookie technology, the multimedia capabilities of the Web allow three-dimensional tours and demonstrations, audio clips, video clips, and real time audio and video streams. These features are ideal for product demonstrations, previews, and step-by-step online instructional support for consumers. American Honda Motor Company, for example, puts Web visitors in a virtual driver's seat with a three-dimensional display that can be manipulated to view the entire interior of various vehicle models.

Another potential marketing tool is the graphical chat interface, such as The Palace.[1] This type of software facilitates a real time chat environment that allows users to see an image of the virtual space in which they're communicating. Each user is represented on the screen by a graphic image called an "avatar," which can be moved and positioned as the user wishes. For example, a homebuilder could create a Palace chat site in which each chat room is a photograph of a room from a model home. Visitors could then visually place themselves within the floor plan, ask questions about new home features, and "visit" the construction site from across the country or around the world.

Investor & Financial Relations on the Internet

Investor and financial relations are major areas of growth on the Internet. Many organizations now routinely use the Web to help increase trading volume and broaden their shareholder bases. Tools for this include Web-based annual reports and financial announcements, stock prices, filings with the U.S. Securities and Exchange Commission (SEC), the prospectus for a proposed merger, and position statements and backgrounders. In addition, electronic news releases inform interested publics of developing financial stories, mergers, acquisitions, or corporate investments as they occur.

Issues Management on the Internet

Chapter 3 described how New Publics emerge on the Internet. This phenomenon is particularly significant in the area of tracking and managing issues. Listservs and other online discussions can be useful ways to monitor developing issues, as well as to offer support to consumers. Specialized searching systems that explore archived Usenet discussions such as DejaNews are especially helpful for this function. DejaNews (`http://www.dejanews.com`) allows keyword searches that describe a client's product or services and retrieves postings from Usenet newsgroups. This allows you to monitor newly forming discussions that may affect the client, as well as identify New Publics during in the early stages of development. Of course, issues management on the Internet requires time, effort, and consistent, long-term, hands-on involvement, in order to be effective.

In addition to surveillance and monitoring of newly emerging issues and publics, Web-based position papers also can be useful. Some organizations devote entire segments of their Web sites to address new or existing issues that affect their relationships with various publics. Unocal, for example, maintains extensive information on its Web site about its corporate responsibility concerning environmental issues, human rights, economic principles, health and safety, and other topical issues.

Education & Outreach on the Internet

The Web is an ideal venue for extending educational messages beyond traditional community boundaries. Local, national, and international not-for-profit organizations provide educational information, volunteer opportunities, event announcements, and donor recognition messages on their Web sites. Chat rooms also offer low-cost peer support groups to people that log in from all over the world.

In addition to traditional Web sites and chat rooms, the graphical interfaces offer new ways to extend educational outreach efforts. For example, a museum or art gallery might utilize The Palace to create chat rooms that represent particular exhibits or museum areas. Visitors could tour with an online "docent" and ask questions. Virtual museums and graphic-intensive Web sites also make use of three-dimensional graphical software to allow Web users to manipulate and view three-dimensional images from a variety of perspectives. The University of Southern California, for example, offers virtual tours of the campus where visitors can stroll down campus avenues, zoom in toward various buildings, and manipulate panoramic views of key areas.[2]

Employee Relations & Employment Opportunities

Many companies now routinely use the Internet or a company-private intranet for employee relations and other internal communications. The reduction of paperwork alone makes electronic communication attractive to managers and line staff alike. Examples of how Internet technology can be used for employee relations include company-wide announcements of training opportunities, special events, changes in policies or procedures, and job openings. For these as for other forms of public relations communications, it's a good idea to use multiple channels. For example, an organizational e-mail announcement might be backed up with a Web page for individuals who inadvertently delete the e-mail version.

In addition to internal employee communications, prospective employees are invited to submit electronic résumés and, in some cases, electronic portfolios for consideration. AirTouch Communications, Inc., for example, accepts electronic résumés both for specific positions and for general consideration. Prospective employees can review company benefits online, then complete an electronic résumé form, write an electronic cover letter, and submit both directly to the organization.[3]

Government Relations on the Internet

The Internet is useful, but not as inclusive for government relations as it is for other public relations endeavors. Certainly, legislators are not likely to visit your Web site to ascertain your opinion on public policy issues. In other words, government relations typically require a pro-active approach to be effective. In addition, some, but not all legislators actively utilize e-mail as a regular form of communication. It therefore pays to check the extent to which you might be able to reach your target audiences through electronic means. A fax or a phone call sometimes is more effective than e-mail. However, those limitations notwithstanding, many organizations are using the Web very effectively for government relations. Various engineering societies, for example, include sections for government relations in their Web sites. One such society, the American Society of Mechanical Engineers, has an extensive section on government relations, which explains, in part:

> ASME International's government relations program is directed at affecting the outcome of issues identified by members as important to the practice of mechanical engineering in the public interest. Under the direction of the Board on Government Relations, the program is conducted through a framework of activities aimed at identifying issues and strategies; informing the ASME membership; involving society members through a variety of programs for individuals and groups; preparing and presenting position statements, testimony, and technical briefs; and holding meetings with policymakers.[4]

The ASME Web site includes position statements, its public policy agenda, information on its legislative action center, its publications and programs, and more.

General Online Public Relations Techniques

Some techniques can be used for several of the public relations functions described in this chapter. For example, you might either work with an advertising department or include some advertising functions in your campaign. That means you might be responsible, in part or in whole, for banner ads that stretch across the top or bottom of a Web site, or box or button ads that may or may not invite users to "click through" to access a Web page specific to the advertisement.

Another technique is the "interstitial"— the pop-up window that sometimes appears when you access a particular Web site. Interstitials usually are enabled by the Java programming language, which was developed by Sun Microsystems to facilitate moving text, window activity, and user interaction. Although they're often used for advertising, interstitials also can feature late-breaking news or other public relations messages.

You also might consider the possibility of either sponsoring Web sites or recruiting sponsors for your Web site in exchange for logo placement or advertising. Procter & Gamble, for example, sponsors an educational site on dental care (http://www.dentalcare.com/), which includes professional continuing education

information, consumer education, information for
faculty, online journals, and more—and features
Procter & Gamble dental products. In addition, a
graphical chat room such as The Palace might be
particularly beneficial for a site of this type,
especially where young audiences are targeted.

A number of search engines are supported through
sponsoring ads, and some Web sites even link
keyword searches to the ads that are displayed with
the search results. For example, the results for a
search of the keyword "wine" on Yahoo may include
a click-through banner ad for Secret Cellars Online
Wine Club and a click-through box ad for The Digital
Chef. (See Figure 6.1.)

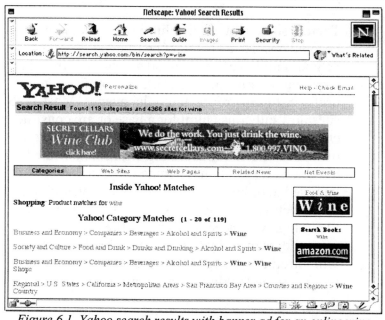

Figure 6.1. Yahoo search results with banner ad for an online wine club with a box ad for The Digital Chef (Digital Chef ad appears on right, above Amazon.com ad).

Finally, the Web, as well as electronic discussion groups can be an excellent tool for rumor control, as we shall see in Chapter 8.

Developing & Launching a Web Presence

Creating a Web site can be daunting at first, but it's really quite manageable. The first thing to do is learn the rudiments of html. This section will first explain how html works, then address some key design issues. Finally, it will discuss some ways to launch your new Web site.

There's some thought that html will eventually become obsolete. That may be true, but the concepts behind html have been around a long time (relatively speaking in terms of the Web), and are likely to be useful in future programming languages. Most Web sites now either use html for a base or are constructed entirely in it. Thus, whether you're authoring your own Web site or collaborating with sophisticated designers, it pays to have some rudimentary knowledge of html and how it works. Even if you're using a current version of a good html editor, you're likely to have a need to change a file name or make a minor adjustment by hand. Therefore, this section will introduce you to html and explain what some of those strange looking codes mean.

Demystifying HTML

Three main concepts characterize html. Once you know them, you can pretty much figure out most of the coding when you look at it.

First, all html codes are embedded in "greater than" and "lesser than" signs:

```
<>
```

The <> signs simply tell your Web browser that anything between them should be read as html code.

Second, most (but not all) html code "turns on" and "turns off" various commands like a toggle. For example, if you want your text to be in italics, you simply place an "I" between the <>. Unlike Internet addresses, the code is not case sensitive, so it can be either upper or lower case. We'll use upper case here, to help distinguish it from the rest of the text:

```
<I>
```

Third, "turning off" the toggle is done by adding a slash before the code between the <>:

```
</I>
```

With just those three concepts, you already know how to make your text italic on a Web page. To italicize a word in the following sentence, for example, you simply add the <I> and </I> immediately before and after the word you want to appear in italics:

```
This is excellent <I>public
relations</I>.
```

The sentence, when viewed through a Web browser, then appears as follows:

This is excellent *public relations*.

Of course, your browser needs to know when it's looking at an html document and when it's not. So all well-written html pages begin with `<HTML>` and end with `</HTML>`.

Similar code pairings appear throughout html documents. For example, the title that appears at the very top of your browser on a Web page (in the center for Netscape and in the upper left corner for Microsoft Internet Explorer) is created by inserting a `<TITLE></TITLE>` pairing just beneath the `<HTML>`. Other tags work similarly, although not all html codes are paired. New paragraphs, for example, can be delineated simply by a `<P>`, and no `</P>` is required (although some automatic editors use both).

Consider the code in Figure 6.1, which outlines a simple Web page. In this example, the code `<BODY BGCOLOR="#FFFFFF">` tells the Web browser that the background color should be white (the color white is represented by the code #FFFFFF). Similarly, the `<IMG SRC="./doggy.gif">` coding tells the Web browser to display a graphic image entitled "doggy.gif" on the Web page.

```
<HTML>
<TITLE>A GIFt for You!</TITLE>
<BODY BGCOLOR="#FFFFFF">
<CENTER>
<H1> Here's a Little GIFt for You!</H1><P>
<P>
<IMG SRC="./doggy.gif">
<P>
<HR SIZE="6">
<FONT SIZE="-2">11 April, 1999</FONT>
</CENTER>
</BODY>
</HTML>
```

Figure 6.1. A simple Web page viewed through a word processor.

The **. /** symbols within the code of Figure 6.1
represent a "relative path," which is a sort of
shorthand that tells the browser where the image file
is stored in relationship to the html file. In this case,
the image file resides in the same directory as the
html document. The <H1></H1> pairing indicates
the browser should display the largest available html
header. The screen shot in Figure 6.2 depicts how the
code and the image appear when viewed through
Netscape.

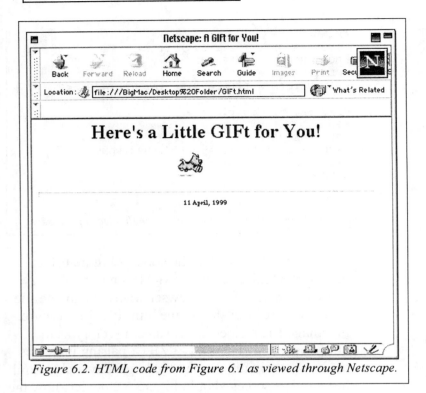

Figure 6.2. HTML code from Figure 6.1 as viewed through Netscape.

Appendix A lists a number of the most commonly
used html tags, along with file extensions you're
likely to see within html documents. One tag that is
important for the public relations practitioner does not
appear in the Table. That is the <META> tag, which
will be addressed later in this chapter.

Designing a Coherent Web Site

Numerous style guides and evaluation resources exist,
both on the Web and off, that can help you with the
design of your site. However, a few key concepts that
are described in this section will help you get started.

First, bear in mind that your Web site is a form of *communication* with target publics. That means you need to keep in mind the general models of communication that were outlined in Chapter 3. Your communication goal is to minimize noise and facilitate clear exchange of ideas between your client and its target publics. Include, for example, a mechanism for the feedback loop. Provide "mailto" hotlinks, e-mail addresses of key staff, telephone numbers, and other appropriate ways for Web users to reach your client. If the client has specific contacts for various functions, be sure the Web site makes very clear whom to contact for each function, including an appropriate contact for comments or questions about the Web site itself.

Second, printed materials, no matter how effective they are in print, don't always translate well to the Web. Both the limitations of html and the ability of users to alter the ways in which the Web site is viewed can create problems for translating printed matter directly to the Web. Don't be afraid to be creative, and to exploit the hypertextual and multimedia features of the Web for the site. A number of researchers have identified various aspects of CMC that are useful in this regard. Sheizaf Rafaeli of the Hebrew University, Jerusalem, Israel was among the first to point out the interactive characteristics of CMC.[5] Incorporating maximum interactivity into your Web site can help engage Web users and encourage them to return. The work of Donna Hoffman and Thomas Novak at Vanderbilt University also can be helpful in this regard. They have drawn on the concept of "flow," which was developed by Mihalyi Csikszentmihalyi (pronounced "chick-sent-mee-high-yee")[6] to explain people's optimal experiences.

Hoffman and Novak described flow, in part, as a balance between feeling challenged and feeling competent and in control. When an ideal balance is reached, a state of "flow" occurs in which the person is fully engaged to the near exclusion of all else.[7] Examples of flow might include becoming so engaged in a hobby or in surfing the Web that the individual loses several unintended hours. Features that might promote a state of flow and incorporate activity include questionnaires for users to complete, contests, downloadable software, real time video and audio streams or archived clips, three-dimensional images that users can manipulate, and sound effects.

Third, before you begin, sketch out a site map of the features and information you expect to include in the Web site. In the research and planning stages, you established your goals and objectives, and you determined what messages or information you needed to include. Now you need to figure out how to present those messages on the Web. Try to think like the Web users who are viewing your site for the first time. What sorts of information are they seeking? How should the information be linked? Is the information complex enough to require that the Web site be searchable? Will you need interactive directories? If one of your goals is to reduce telephone-based customer support, you might consider an "infobot," which is an automated program that can e-mail responses to specific questions or keywords a Web user might send through a Web-based form or e-mail inquiry.

Fourth, double check that the client's staff is both prepared and able to respond quickly to e-mail messages. If the client fails to meet the expectations of Internet users through slow or inadequate responses, the Web site is likely to be more harmful than helpful to the client's reputation.

Fifth, incorporate overall coherence by including a visual identifier on every page and using consistent design schemes throughout the Web site. This is especially important if the site includes hotlinks to external sites, because your design consistency can help users identify when they are accessing pages on your site or on another site.

Sixth, provide easy navigation for users to access any area of your site with a minimum of clicking. This means thinking through how you want material presented. For example, if you have a section content that should be presented sequentially, the pages in that section might include simple "back" and "next" buttons. However, you also want to give users an opportunity to move from that section to any other section of your Web site with a simple click of the mouse. This usually means that you'll want to include a navigation bar of some sort. In addition, access assisted by search engines frequently results in a user accessing your site at a low-level page rather than the "home" page. This emphasizes the need for making navigation easy and accessible from all areas of the Web site.

Seventh, give some thought to the ways in which Web users will access and utilize your site, and make appropriate adjustments to the design. Just because you *can* do something doesn't always mean you *should*. Frames, for example, can render bookmarks ineffective, and if the frames are not well designed, they can also create navigational problems. If you want the material to be printable, consider a light background and dark text, and avoid Java and JavaScript features that do not print. This concept also affects the way the site is constructed, in terms of depth or shallowness of menus. Strive for a reasonable balance of content and navigational features that will minimize excessive scrolling through many screens full of text but also will not result in users being forced to click through endless submenus.

Eighth, avoid overusing graphic elements, and use images of similar sizes and characteristics, placing them with as much care on a Web page as you would on a printed page. This will help avoid a disjointed and cluttered appearance that Patrick Lynch of Yale University and Sarah Horton of Dartmouth College call "clown's pants." [8] Remember that graphics and text should work together to convey your message to your target publics, and should draw the viewer's eye to the essential components of the message. Similarly, typography should be consistent and easy to read, using only one or two compatible families of typefaces.

Ninth, use the same criteria for designing your Web site that you use for evaluating them. For example, as indicated in Chapter 4, *currency* is an important aspect of high-quality Web-based information. This means that good Web design includes letting the user know how up-to-date the information is, and incorporating a date of creation or revision on every page.

Finally, make the site as flexible as you can to accommodate the widest possible range of users. Different users will access your Web site from different computers and through all sorts of systems.

They may not have your browser, your screen size, your screen resolution, your connection speed, or even your operating system. If your site is heavy in graphics, for example, you'll probably need to include alternate text messages and use interlaced[9] images wherever possible to allow users with slow modems to determine if they want to wait for the graphic elements to load. Similarly, if you're using a specialized font, include an alternative in the html code to display the text as Times, Helvetica, or Courier. That will enable viewers to read the text where they might otherwise see only meaningless generic characters. For example, if you use Arial as the font for body text on your page, Helvetica is a reasonable alternate font. The html code, then, would appear as:

```
<FONT FACE="Arial,Helvetica>
```

Writing for a Web Site

Writing the text for a Web site is much like any other public relations writing project. The challenge is to draw the reader into your message. That means you need to follow many of the same guidelines you would follow for other types of PR writing, and also bear in mind that the text will be read on a computer screen. The following ten basic tips will help you write effectively for the Web:

1. As with all effective public relations writing, your text must be mechanically excellent, and free of any grammar, punctuation, spelling, or syntax errors.
2. Avoid "puff" words, clichés, and exaggerations.

3. Keep the sentences short, crisp, and to the point (approximately 16 words or so).
4. Use active verbs and avoid passive voice.
5. Support main ideas with proper evidence.
6. Keep individual paragraphs focused on one central idea.
7. Make sure each paragraph logically follows the one before it.
8. Set the reading level appropriate to the readership; use short words and sentences for young or inexperienced readers.
9. Avoid a patronizing tone by talking "with" rather than "at" the reader.
10, Avoid jargon, acronyms, and other specialized language that may confuse the reader.

Review your text for accuracy and readability. If necessary, test to make sure your message is clear, and that it is easily understood on a computer screen. Remember that the text and the graphics should work together to create a coherent message.

Of course, once you've built your Web site, there's no guarantee that people will visit it. You'll also need to do some public relations for your public relations effort and launch the site.

Hints for Launching the Web site

Before launching the Web site, you can avoid a variety unforeseen problems by "test driving" it with a variety of computers and through a variety of browsers, including various versions of browsers. Some methods for testing the site's accessibility, navigability, readability, and comprehensibility include pilot testing with a representative sample of users, focus groups, and split sample tests with alternative site designs. Once you know the site is stable, the server is operational, and all the links are working well, you're ready to launch the site.

Domain Names

One of the first things that can help launch a successful Web site is the domain name. Registering a unique domain name can help establish a visible presence on the Web and increase name recognition. There are a variety of services that will handle the filing of new domain names for nominal charges, but you also can file directly through InterNIC,® which is a cooperative activity between the U.S. Government and Network Solutions, Inc.[10] Although registration is not expensive, "dot-com" domain names are becoming scarce, so some institutions now are using the two-character country extension for the U.S.

Search Engines: Registration & Maintenance

Search engines probably constitute the most often used tool for launching Web sites. Many services exist that will, for a fee, register your site with a variety of engines. However, if you have the time and patience, you can register your site without payment of a fee by filling out Web-based forms for each search engine with which you'd like to include your. Each service requires slightly different information, and each has a different policy on the types of sites it will accept.

Registration with search engines, much like a Web site itself, requires some maintenance. Competition is keen to keep Web sites among the first 40 or 50 to be retrieved by major search engines. When your site is freshly listed, it is likely to come up fairly quickly when people use a searching system. However, as the registration ages, your site may be buried among hundreds of other sites that the search terms retrieve. Since most people tend to look at only a few pages of "hits," it pays to keep your site listing fresh.

One way to improve your chances of meaningful retrievals through searching and indexing systems, and to help make your site accessible to search engine "spiders" is to use a <META> tag near the top of the html document. Web browsers do not display the text of <META> tags, but many search engines' documenting and retrieval systems read them for content or keywords. Changing the <META> tags frequently can help keep your site fresh with search and indexing systems. For example, a <META> tag for the American Red Cross during the NATO operation in Yugoslavia and the crisis over Kosovo read:

```
<HTML>
<META name="description" content="The
American Red Cross helps keep people
safe every day as well as in an
emergency thanks to caring people who
support our work in the community.
Please support your local Red Cross">
<META name="keywords" content="Kosovo,
Serb, Albania, Macedonia, soldiers,
military, Yugoslavia, refugee, Geneva
Convention, airstrikes, Cohen, airlift,
NATO, Prisoners of War, Pentagon,
atrocities, twister, tornado, midwest,
```

Montgomery, Ohio, Louisiana, Massacre,
Nicaragua, Colombia, volunteer,
humanitarian, donor, blood, CPR, safety,
charity, health, Elizabeth Dole, Wynonna
Judd, January, February, March is Red
Cross Month, April, May, June, July,
August, September, October, November,
December, calendar, video, multimedia,
CPR/AED, Automated External
Defibrillator, plasma, biomedical,
stemcells, tissue, Monarc-M,
Panglobulin, Polygam S/D, Albumarc,
dental, pet first aid, plateletpheresis,
help, donate, current events, service,
donations, emergency, disaster, HIV,
AIDS, refugee, world, international,
tracing, education, courses, prepare,
preparedness, landmines, flood, tornado,
earthquake, hurricane, snow, y2k,
blizzard, landslide, fire, storm,
mudslide, cyclone, family, child,
community, military, Red Cross, Red
Crescent, IFRC, ICRC">[11]

The Red Cross example illustrates both keywords that
are generally characteristic of the Red Cross
organization and services, and terms that are specific
to Red Cross international humanitarian activities
during a particular crisis. However, not all search
engines utilize <META> tags. Some index full text of
pages; others rely on human verification. Therefore, it
also pays to keep your site content fresh, accurate,
and up-to-date.

Access Registration Procedures

Consider the possibility of fine-tuning your
understanding of your online publics by incorporating

a registration procedure into your Web site. By
having people register to access your site, you can
gather demographic and psychographic information
as part of the registration process. This will help you
evaluate your site after it's been launched, as well as
help you develop and implement Web site appropriate
improvements to communicate effectively with your
online target publics.

Chapter Summary

Using the Internet to prepare and deliver public
relations messages requires an understanding both of
the process of communication and of the medium. It
is therefore critical for practitioners to follow the
rules of good "netiquette" for simultaneous and
nonsimultaneous communications. Tips for beginners
on the 'Net include: 1) reading FAQs, 2) lurking to
learn online group norms, 3) using "Internet style" in
e-mail by avoiding all caps, which are considered
"shouting," and limiting signatures to four lines
4) avoiding "spam," 5) including identification
appropriate to the online group, 6) keeping messages
short, 7) minimizing in-text quotation, 8) using proper
commands and sending them to the proper places to
sign off or change settings on an e-mail discussion
list, 9) using appropriate spelling and grammar, and
10) avoiding the spread of rumors, hoaxes, and urban
legends.

Public relations uses of the Internet include both
simultaneous and nonsimultaneous forms of CMC for
media relations, consumer relations and marketing,
investor and financial relations, issues management,

education and outreach, employee relations and
employment opportunities, and government relations.

Developing and launching a Web site require careful
thought in light of general communication models
and rudimentary understanding of html. Nearly all
html coding is embedded in <> and most of it is in
pairs of <></> to toggle effects "on" and "off." Ten
pointers can help guide Web site development:
1) include a feedback loop; 2) incorporate
interactivity into the Web design; 3) develop a site
map that depicts the information to be conveyed and
how users can access it; 4) make sure the client's staff
can handle the volume of e-mail generated by the
Web site; 5) Use identifiers, logos, and consistent
design schemes throughout the Web site; 6) include
navigation tools on all pages of the site; 7) limit
design features to those that will be useful for your
particular users; 8) avoid overuse of graphic elements
and elements that disrupt the overall coherence of a
page; 9) use the same criteria for designing a Web site
that you use for evaluating one; and 10) make the site
as flexible as possible to accommodate a maximum
variety of user systems.

Web sites require thoughtful launching and
maintenance to be effective. Consider the possibility
of a unique domain name to increase the client's
name recognition, and register the site with search
engines. The use of <META> tags can help increase
visibility and retrievability with some search engines.

Exercises

1. Reflect on an e-mail discussion list or Usenet newsgroup to which you belong. If you don't belong to one, you can visit a Usenet newsgroup through the "news" feature of your Web browser. Does it have an orientation posting or an FAQ? What information does the FAQ include? Do you see evidence of the rules that are outlined in the document? Based on the postings, do you think the members of the list would "flame" someone who violated the rules or norms? Why or why not?

2. Visit at least five corporate and five not-for-profit Web sites (ten in all). On a piece of paper, write down whether each of the sites includes a section for each of the following functions:

   a) Media relations.
   b) Consumer and relations.
   c) Marketing.
   d) Investor and financial relations.
   e) Issues management.
   f) Education and outreach.
   g) Employee relations and employment opportunities.
   h) Government relations.

3. For each of the Web sites you visited in #2 above, use the "view" menu of your browser to view the source code of the page. Does the code include <META> tags? What types of keywords do the tags use?

4. Armed with the keywords you find in the
   <META> tags in #3 above, visit one of the search
   engines listed in the Notes at the end of Chapter 4.
   Type in the keywords from the <META> tags.
   Does the search engine retrieve the Web site you
   visited within the first 40 "hits" ? If not, how do
   you think Web designer could improve the
   retrieval rate?

5. Try your hand at writing some html. Use the code
   in Table 6.1 to get started. Add any GIF you like
   instead of the "doggy.gif." Try embellishing
   the page, using the tags shown in Appendix A as
   reference. Be sure to save your document as "text
   only," but use a one-word file name (no spaces or
   unusual characters) with the ".html" extension.
   You can then launch a Web browser to view it
   periodically as you work.

References

AirTouch Communications, Inc. (1998). *AirTouch Human Resources Employment Opportunities.* Available:
http://www.app.airtouch.com/index_employment.html

American Society of Mechanical Engineers. (no date). *Overview of ASME Government Relations.* In ASME: Government Relations. Available:
http://www.asme.org/gric/about.html

American Honda Motor Company, Inc. (1998). *Honda Automobiles|1999 Model Year.* Available:
http://www.honda1999.com/

American Red Cross. (1999). *American Red Cross.* Available:
http://www.redcross.org/

Csikszentmihalyi, M. (1975). *Beyond boredom and anxiety.* San Francisco: Jossey-Bass.

Csikszentmihalyi, M. (1990). *Flow: The psychology of optimal experience.* New York: HarperCollins.

Csikszentmihalyi, M. (1993). *The evolving self: A psychology for the third millennium.* New York: HarperCollins.

Csikszentmihalyi, M. & Selega-Csikszentmihalyi, I. (Eds.). (1989). *Optimal experience: Psychological studies of flow in consciousness.* New York: Cambridge University Press.

Electric Communities. (1999). *The Palace Visual Chat|Home Page*. Available:
http://www.thepalace.com/

Hoffman, D. L., & Novak, T. P. (1996), Marketing in computer-mediated environments: Conceptual foundations. *Journal of Marketing, 60*. 50-68.

Lynch, P. J., & Horton, S. (1997). *Yale Center for Advanced Instructional Media Web Style Guide*. Available:
http://info.med.yale.edu/caim/manual/contents.html

Rafaeli, S. (1988). Interactivity. In R. P. Hawkins, J. M. Wiemann, and S. Pingree (Eds.), *Advances in Communication Science: Merging mass and interpersonal processes* (pp. 110-134). Newbury Park, CA: Sage.

Rafaeli, S. (1990). Interacting with media: Para-social interaction and real interaction. In B. D. Ruben and L. A. Lievrouw (Eds.), *Mediation, information, and communication: Information and behavior* (Vol. 3) (pp. 125-181). New Brunswick, NJ: Transaction.

Unocal. (no date). *Unocal Web Site: Unocal Corporate Responsibility*. Available:
http://www.unocal.com/responsibility/index.htm

USC School of Cinema-Television. (no date). *VR Tour*. Available:
http://www.usc.edu/dept/TommyCam/newtour.html

Notes

[1] Information about client and server software for The Palace is available at http://www.thepalace.com

[2] USC School of Cinema-Television. (no date). *VR Tour*. Available:
http://www.usc.edu/dept/TommyCam/newtour.html

[3] AirTouch Communications, Inc. (1998). *AirTouch Human Resources Employment Opportunities*. Available:
http://www.app.airtouch.com/index_employment.html

[4] American Society of Mechanical Engineers. (no date). *Overview of ASME Government Relations*. In ASME: Government Relations. Available:
http://www.asme.org/gric/about.html

[5] Rafaeli, S. (1988). Interactivity. In R. P. Hawkins, J. M. Wiemann, and S. Pingree (Eds.), *Advances in Communication Science: Merging mass and interpersonal processes* (pp. 110-134). Newbury Park, CA: Sage.

[6] Csikszentmihalyi, M. (1990). *Flow: The psychology of optimal experience*. New York: Harper & Row.

[7] Hoffman, D. L., & Novak, T. P. (1996), Marketing in computer-mediated environments: Conceptual foundations. *Journal of Marketing, 60.* 50-68.

[8] Lynch, P. J., & Horton, S. (1997). Page design: Graphic Design 100. In *Yale Center for Advanced Instructional Media Web Style Guide*. Available:
http://info.med.yale.edu/caim/manual/pages/graphic_design100.html

[9] Interlacing refers to a form of GIF that allows an entire image to load as a matrix that fills in, rather than as a full-color, line-by-line image. An interlaced image appears in its entirety on the screen although it appears faded until it is fully loaded. As it continues to load, the viewer is able to read the text of the page. This is especially useful for users with slower modems who want to access the page content without waiting for entire images to load.

[10] InterNIC. (no date) *Thanks for visiting www.internic.net!* Available: http://www.networksolutions.com/internic/internic.html

[11] American Red Cross. (1999, April). *Torn from homes, separated from families.* Online: http://www.redcross.org/

Chapter 7. Evaluation

The Fourth Step

Learning Objectives

This chapter addresses the fourth step of the public relations process, evaluation. Major topics covered in the next few pages include:

➢ Measurement techniques for evaluating public relations activities, programs, and campaigns.
➢ The Internet as an evaluation tool.
➢ Methods for evaluating your Internet-based programs and campaigns.

Measurement Techniques for Public Relations

Evaluation, the last step of the public relations process, helps us determine the extent to which we met our objectives, measure our progress toward overall organizational and public relations goals, and identify areas for improvement. For that reason, although most evaluation is done after a campaign or program has been completed, you really need to establish the measures you will use during the second, planning step of the four-step public relations process.

Recall that Chapter 5 described well-written objectives as being specific, *measurable*, and bound by time. Therefore, this step and the second step of the four-step process are tightly linked. In the second step, you planned the evaluation techniques to be used; in this step, you implement your evaluation plan. Similarly, the evaluation step is linked with the first phase of the four-step process, because evaluation of what worked and what didn't forms the basis for future activities and provides information from which you can draw as you begin the research for another campaign or program.

In evaluation, as in the other steps of the public relations process, we can see how the structures of the technology and of the human interactions with and through that technology both constrain and enable our communication efforts. For example, computer "cookies" can help us track a viewer's progress through a Web site, but can mislead us if the computer is one used by several different people.

Types of Measurements for Communication

The specific forms of evaluation we use depend on the questions we want to answer. Sometimes, we need to provide activity reports to a manager or client. That means we need to be able to measure our productivity. Other times, we want to know things like how many people could potentially have seen a message, or if people could recall the message, or if they understood the message, or if they behaved in a particular way as a result of the message. Each type of question requires a different type of measurement and evaluation. We can probably categorize public relations evaluation techniques into five general categories, which are based on the questions we ask:

1. Measurements of productivity.
2, Measurements of message distribution and exposure.
3. Measurements of audience receipt.
4. Measurements of comprehension.
5. Measurements of attitude or behavior change.

Measurements of Productivity

Productivity measurements help us provide management with an idea of our activities. Although these measures tend to emphasize quantity over quality, they often are helpful for justifying the need for organizational resources, such as equipment, personnel, or program expenditures. Measurements of productivity simply count the number of specific activities that were accomplished in a particular period, such as how many news releases were distributed in a given month.

Measurements of Message Distribution & Exposure

Measurements of message distribution and exposure provide information on how many messages potentially or actually reached target publics. These techniques do not examine whether messages were understood or accepted, but rather the extent to which they were distributed to target publics. These types of measurements include such bedrock techniques as press clippings, media impressions, and cost per person.

Measurements of Audience Receipt

Measurements of audience receipt determine if target publics have received public relations messages. Although measurements of message distribution and exposure are important, they don't provide information about the extent to which target publics have actually noticed them. Press clippings, for example, are good measures of acceptance by media gatekeepers, but do not tell you if anyone actually *read* your stories. Other measures, such as compiling lists of requests or responses that arise from a story give us a better feeling for how well our messages reached our target publics.

Measurements of Comprehension

Measurements of audience comprehension offer a higher level of analysis than either measures of distribution and exposure or of audience receipt. These measurements focus on whether the target publics actually received the messages you sent, if they were they understood, and if they were they retained. Typically, this form of evaluation is done through survey research.

Measurements of Attitude or Behavior Change

Measurements of attitude or behavior change are established similarly to comprehension measurements. Like those measures, they often rely on benchmark (baseline) studies (pre-tests) prior to the campaign or program and post-tests afterward. The goal, here, is to measure any shift in attitude that may arise from the campaign. Measurements of behavior change focus on the ultimate objective of any campaign or program—boosts in sales, donations, or legislative changes.

These five categories by no means represent every possible form of evaluation we use in the field of public relations. However, they offer a starting point for thinking about the questions you or your client might ask to evaluate the effectiveness of your work. Here, as in the other steps of the public relations process, the Internet can offer some useful tools.

Using the Internet for Evaluation

The Internet can be a useful tool for partial evaluation of an offline public relations campaign. One of the most often used forms of evaluation is the Web-based questionnaire, which surveys visitors to a Web site. Inclusion of URLs on business cards and other printed materials and special promotions can help motivate respondents to participate in online surveys for baseline and comparison studies, reader comprehension of test messages, and other traditional evaluation techniques. In addition, electronic clipping services, like electronic news releases, are changing both the speed and practitioners' expectations of how information is exchanged. A variety of online resources exist to help the practitioner develop and conduct evaluation on the Internet. Beyond that, of course, evaluation techniques are becoming increasingly sophisticated for Web- and Internet-based public relations materials and programs, although they still tend to have several weaknesses.

Evaluating Internet-Based Programs & Campaigns

Internet technologies are making new inroads every day to help the practitioner evaluate Web sites and other online programs and campaigns. Like traditional evaluation techniques, Internet-based methods can be sorted into the five measurements of: 1) productivity, 2) message distribution and exposure, 3) audience receipt, 4) comprehension, and 5) attitude or behavior change. The practitioner faces both new opportunities and new challenges when working with each type of evaluation on the Internet.

Measurements of Productivity

Measures of productivity on the Web, like those off the Web, involve determining the quantitative output of the public relations practitioner. Techniques for using these types of measures can include counting how many e-mail messages were prepared or sent, or how many contacts were made. The job often can be automated by using e-mail-handling programs that allow the user to create different "mailboxes" or files for different types of e-mail and display how many messages are in each in- or out-box.

Measurements of Message Distribution & Exposure

Message distribution and exposure on the Internet is very difficult to establish with any accuracy, especially through Usenet newsgroups or e-mail discussion lists. Although it is possible to review lists of members for some e-mail distribution lists and newsgroups, you really can't ascertain with any certainty how many individuals might see a message distributed through those means. The likelihood of underestimating impressions is huge, because a single member of a list or group might be a FidoNet BBS, which redistributes the message to a membership that may be several hundred strong.

Advertisers are beginning to use page impressions and CPM (cost per thousand of page impressions), but, similar to print, there's no guarantee that a user actually reads your message if they access your page. However, counting "hits" to a Web site and estimated page impressions are obvious online techniques for measuring message exposure to target publics. If you use this sort of technique, you should keep in mind three features of the technology that make truly accurate determination of impressions nearly impossible:

1. Multiple users often use the same computer.
2. Page views may not include the public relations message in question.
3. Browser cache files may store the Web pages that may have previously been visited.

Measurements of Audience Receipt

Similar to measurements of distribution and exposure, measurements of audience receipt can be difficult to gauge on the Internet. If you can't determine how many people to whom messages are distributed, it's even harder to determine how many people have received them. In spite of the limitations of these types of measurements, though, they can help you determine if target publics are seeing your Web site or reading your newsgroup postings. Thus, e-mail responses to a particular story (again stored in separate e-mail boxes for ease of tabulation) can help you determine for how well your messages reached your target publics.

Clearly, simple "hit" counting is severely limited as an effective evaluation technique, and may be misleading. A more sophisticated technique incorporates the use of setting "cookies," which are described in Chapter 3, on a user's browser cache file. Cookies are widely used in organizational Web sites, often in ways that are not readily apparent to the user. They allow you to track the movements of a user through your Web site, tell you the general location of the user's computer for demographic analysis, determine how long a user views a particular page, and provide other useful information.

Measurements of Comprehension

Web-based surveys can help you determine the extent to which target publics actually received and understood your public relations messages. Questionnaires of this nature serve not only to gather information, but also to let your target publics know that you're interested in their perceptions. In addition, they add interactivity to your Web site. The resulting information can be entered automatically into statistical software for analysis.

When conducting Web-based surveys, determining accurate response rates can be difficult, for the same reasons that make measures of distribution and receipt troublesome. Multiple users may use the same computer, a particular page view may not include your public relations message, and browser cache files may prevent your system from recording a bona fide "hit" to your Web site.

In contrast to Web surveys, e-mail based questionnaires tend to be relatively difficult to administer and analyze. They typically have low response rates[1] and, unlike traditional

paper-and-pencil instruments, users can alter the
e-mail questionnaires.

Measurements of Attitude or Behavior Change

In spite of their weaknesses, Web-based
questionnaires can be very helpful in measuring
attitude or behavior changes that result from public
relations activities on the Internet. Since the goal is to
measure any shift in attitude that may arise from the
online portion of a campaign, both online and offline
measures are appropriate for evaluating attitude or
opinion changes.

Behavior changes, like message comprehension, can
be measured with online surveys, especially if your
Web site offers electronic means for purchase or
donation. Here, you would record and analyze trends
in online sales or donations. However, since some
people tend to "window shop" on the Web then make
purchases in more traditional ways like phone, mail
order, or in-store shopping, these techniques should
be combined with similar measurements through a
variety of media and methods.

Chapter Summary

Evaluation is the last step of the public relations
process, and helps us determine the extent to which
we met our objectives, measure our progress toward
overall organizational and public relations goals, and
identify areas for improvement. Public relations

measurement techniques typically fall into one of five categories: 1) measurements of productivity, 2) measurements of message distribution and exposure, 3) measurements of audience receipt, 4) measurements of comprehension, and 5) measurements of attitude or behavior change.

The structures of the technology and of the human interactions with and through that technology both constrain and enable evaluation efforts in and of online public relations. Electronic press clippings, cookies, cost per thousand page views, and online questionnaires are a few examples of measurement methods being used on the Internet.

Exercises

1. Conduct a keyword search for questionnaires or surveys, and then access any corporate Web site that has an online questionnaire. What types of information is the questionnaire trying to elicit from respondents? Can you identify which of the five categories described in this chapter the information is intended to address?

   a) Measurements of productivity.
   b) Measurements of message distribution and exposure.
   c) Measurements of audience receipt.
   d) Measurements of comprehension.
   e) Measurements of attitude or behavior change.

2. Visit two or three of the search engine Web sites listed in the Notes of Chapter 4. Conduct a keyword search for "beer," one for "computers," and one for "toys." Notice which advertisements appear on your screen with the results for each. How do they differ?

References

Marlow, E. (1996). *Electronic public relations.* Belmont, CA: Wadsworth.

Pitkow, J. E. & Recker, M. M. (1994). Results from the First World-Wide Web User Survey. Available: http://www.gatech.edu/pitkow/survey/survey.html

Rich. C. (1999). *Creating online media: A guide to research, writing and design on the internet.* Boston: McGraw-Hill College.

Witmer, D. F., Colman, R. W., & Katzman, S. L. (1999). From paper-and-pencil to screen-and-keyboard: Toward a methodology for survey research on the Internet. In S. Jones (Ed.). *Doing Internet Research.* (pp. 145-161). Newbury Park, CA: Sage.

Notes

[1] Pitkow, J. E. & Recker, M. M. (1994). Results from the First World-Wide Web User Survey. Available: http://www.gatech.edu/pitkow/survey/survey.html

Chapter 8. Special Uses of the Internet

Crisis Communication, Rumor Control, & More

Learning Objectives

This chapter describes cases that illustrate excellence in public relations using the Internet. Specific examples in this chapter include:

➢ Federal Express: customer support.
➢ NASA: education and outreach.
➢ Swissair: crisis communication.
➢ Procter & Gamble: rumor control.

Special Cases of Public Relations on the Internet

We've already looked at a broad variety of ways that the Internet can be used for the practice of public relations. This chapter will address some specific cases that illustrate specialized uses of CMC to meet public relations goals.

Federal Express: Customer Support

FedEx is one of the first organizations to have incorporated the Internet into its daily operations and its customer services. The shipping firm handles more than 55 million pounds of airfreight each month, and processes 63 million electronic transactions every day.[1]

Since 1995, FedEx has offered individuals and businesses FedEx Ship,® a free software package that enables placement of shipping orders, printing of air bills, and tracking services. In 1996, the company also launched its interNetShip,® which enables businesses and individuals to request a parcel pickup, track a shipment, print air bill labels, and request invoice adjustments. Package recipients can request e-mail notification of a package shipment.

A report on The Emerging Digital Economy by the U.S. Department of Commerce indicates that within

18 months of launching interNetShip, 75,000 FedEx customers had adopted it as a means of communicating with FedEx. Customers soon were tracking more than one million packages each month through interNetShip.

The benefits of using the Internet for customer services were evident both for FedEx and for its customers. Web use reduced costs for the company because roughly half of the tracking that was done through the Internet would have been handled through the FedEx toll-free telephone lines. It also improved customer perception of the Federal Express support services, because customers could choose to contact the company by phone, fax, or electronic means. Nearly 950,000 of them found electronic contact to be the most convenient method.[2]

As a result of the increasing use of the Internet to provide customer support and services, business-to-business organizations that help facilitate customer support services are emerging. Net Effect Systems, Inc., for example, is a software development company headquartered in North Hollywood, California. The company's primary focus is development of software and services that enable companies to establish real time Internet-based e-commerce, customer services, and technical support. Net Effect is part of a Customer Support Consortium, which is a non-profit alliance of organizations that provide technical support products and services. A major development of the Consortium is its Solution-Centered Support™ model, which "focuses on capturing, sharing and reusing solutions to leverage knowledge."[3] In essence, this means that when a customer service requires a person-generated e-mail response, the response is then used to generate improvements to the automated database support system.

NASA: Education & Outreach

The National Aeronautics and Space Administration strategic plan includes a focus on education to "involve the educational community in our endeavors to inspire America's students, create learning opportunities, and enlighten inquisitive minds."[4] The Web plays a major role in making NASA educational programs accessible to students and educators. In fact, NASA centers offer not just one, but twelve field center educational Web sites, in addition to the headquarters educational site.[5]

The NASA headquarters educational Web site offers, among other features, a searchable database of its educational programs, interactive, instructional videos and web-based programs, real time video streams, calendars, and news updates, and other resources for teachers and students. The Spacelink online multimedia center, in particular, capitalizes on the Web's multimedia capabilities to deliver three-dimensional images and models, interactive models that students can manipulate, real time video feeds of missions and projects, and more.

Swissair: Crisis Communication

On the night of September 3, 1998 Swissair flight
SR111 went down off the coast of Peggy's Cove,
Nova Scotia at 10:31 local Canadian time. The flight
had left New York's John F. Kennedy Airport two
hours and thirteen minutes earlier, and was bound for
Geneva. No one aboard survived. A total of 215
passengers and 14 crew were lost. [6]

As has been the case in a number of high-profile air
disasters, the cause of the accident was a mystery, and
a lengthy investigation was launched. Swissair also
immediately implemented its crisis communication
plan, which involved extensive use of the Internet. By
9:30 A.M. Central European Time, six hours after the
accident, Swissair had distributed the news release
that appears in Figure 8.1.

Because Zürich-based Swissair is an international
carrier and flight SR111 involved three countries (the
U.S.A. departure, the Canadian accident site, and the
Swiss destination), the Internet was an excellent
vehicle to reach appropriate target publics.

The Swissair communication did not stop at news
releases. As Figure 8.1 indicates, Swissair
immediately launched into a multidimensional
communication program. Activities during this period
included publication of toll-free dedicated phone lines
for family members, sending professionals to Geneva
to counsel relatives of the victims, posting a Web-
based form that friends and relatives could use to fax
inquiries, and making sure Swissair presence and
concern was evident at the investigation site.

Press Release - 09:30 AM (CET)

Swissair aircraft involved in accident

Zurich, September 3, 1998 - A Swissair aircraft crashed off the coast of Nova Scotia, Canada at 03:20 this morning (Central European Time). The aircraft, an MD-11, was operating flight SR 111 from New York to Geneva, and was carrying 215 passengers and 14 crew.

The aircraft had taken off from New York's John F. Kennedy Airport at 20:18 (local time) and was due to lard in Geneva at 09:30 this morning (local time). Shortly before Halifax, Canada, the crew reported smoke in the cockpit and attempted an emergency landing at Halifax Airport. About 30 miles south of the airport, the aircraft disappeared from radar screens.

Search and rescue operations are currently under way. Aircraft, helicopters and rescue vessels are searching for survivors, though only wreckage has so far been found.

Dedicated phone lines have been established for the relatives involved. A team of specially-trained personnel has also been provided at Geneva to assist and counsel relatives.

Relatives' contact numbers:
New York: (1) 800 801 0088
Zurich: (41 1) 803 1717
Geneva: (41 22) 717 8300

Media contact: (41 1) 812 7117

Figure 8.1. Swissair media release.[7]

News was breaking fast. As a result, Swissair distributed four news releases within the first twelve hours after the accident, including a release announcing immediate compensation to family

members. This meant that a global audience, anxious
for news from the airline, was accessing the Swissair
Web site, often every few minutes, for updates.
Knowing that Web browsers would retain cache files
that would prevent viewers from seeing the updated
information, Swissair posted the following notice in
red type on the Web pages devoted to SR111:

> Please use SHIFT + RELOAD / REFRESH to get
> the latest version of this and following pages.

The speed of Internet transmission helped Swissair
communicate quickly and effectively with its target
publics in an crisis situation. However, the nature of
computer-mediated communication could have
created even more problems for the beleaguered
airline, had it not understood both the advantages
and disadvantages of the technology.

Procter & Gamble: Rumor Control

Procter & Gamble, like a number of other corporate
entities, has had to battle a variety of rumors
throughout the years. One such rumor, which was
circulated on the Internet, targeted a new product
called Febreze, which is designed to remove pet,
smoke, cooking, and other deeply embedded odors
from fabrics. The rumor indicated that Febreze was
not safe to use around dogs, cats, and birds because it
contained zinc chloride.[8]

In response to the rumor, Procter & Gamble acted
quickly, and created an area on the Febreze Web site
that is devoted to "Pet Safety." The Web page
conforms to good public relations practices by not

repeating the rumor verbatim, but by referring to it and then providing information from credible sources to refute it. The Web site begins as follows:

> If you've reached this page, chances are you've received an e-mail chain letter warning you about using Febreze around your pets. These rumors simply are not true. Used as directed, Febreze is safe to use around pets. Nevertheless, we're glad you stopped by to get the facts![9]

The Web page cites the American Society for the Prevention of Cruelty to Animals (ASPCA), which states, in part, "All information reviewed to date suggests that there is no evidence that Febreze represents any risk to pets when used according to label instructions." Procter & Gamble also provides evidence that Febreze is safe, and includes hotlinks to the ASPCA, the Veterinary Emergency Center in Needham, MA, and other related Web sites, including some that specialize in Internet hoaxes. In addition, the Febreze Web site offers a consumer FAQ, which answers questions about the product, its contents, and its safety.

Because the rumor was propagated on the Internet, the Procter & Gamble Web site is especially appropriate. In fact, as we will see in Chapter 9, hoaxes and urban legends abound on the 'Net.

Chapter Summary

This chapter described four cases where organizations utilized the Internet to attain public relations goals. Federal Express maintains two-way communication with target publics through online customer services and support. NASA provides information and services to educators and students through its online education program. The Swissair case illustrates excellence in crisis communications and the role the Internet can play in communicating with target publics. Procter & Gamble neutralizes rumors by providing accurate and well-supported information on its Web site. Each of these four brief cases exemplifies ways in which well-thought-out use of the Internet can enhance public relations.

Exercises

1. Visit the Baltimore Gas & Electric educational
    resources Web site at
    http://www.bge.com/newsinfo/edures/cp.htm

    a) What resources for educators can you find?
    b) Is the site easily navigated? Why or why not?
    c) Do you think this site is effective as an
        educational resource? Why or why not?
    d) What public relations function does this
        educational site serve for BGE?

2. Think about a school or company with which you
    are familiar. Does it use the Web for public
    relations? If so, visit and explore the Web site.
    Which PR functions does it serve?

3. Does the organizational Web site you visited in
    number 2 above use any other forms of Internet
    communication (e.g., a discussion list or a chat
    room)? How might they help the public relations
    efforts of the organization?

References

Barnett, H. (1999). Principle, HB Marketing
Communications, Brea, CA. Personal Interview,
April 19, 1999.

Federal Express. (1998). FedEX | U.S. Home.
Available:
http://www.fedex.com/us/

Margherio, L., Henry, D., Cooke, S., Montes, S., &
Hughes, K. (1998, April). The emerging digital
economy. U.S. Department of Commerce, National
Technical Information Service. Available:
http://www.ecommerce.gov/emerging.htm

NASA. (1999). NASA Headquarters Education
Program. Available:
http://education.nasa.gov/

Net Effect Systems, Inc. (1998). Welcome to Net
Effect Systems. Available:
http://www.neteffect.com

Procter & Gamble (1998). Febreze - Safely cleans
away odors on fabrics. Available:
http://www.febreze.com/

Swissair (no date) Information about the accident of
SR111. Available:
http://www.swissair.com/info111.htm

Notes

[1] Federal Express. (1998). Who is FedEx? Available:
http://www.fedex.com/us/about/facts.html

[2] Margherio, L., Henry, D., Cooke, S., Montes, S., & Hughes, K. (1998, April). The emerging digital economy. U.S. Department of Commerce, National Technical Information Service. Appendix 3, pp. 8-10. Available:
http://www.ecommerce.gov/Append3.pdf

[3] Net Effect Systems, Inc. (1999). Net Effect Systems: Press release: March 5, 1999. Available:
http://www.neteffect.com/news/pr/990305.html

[4] NASA. (1999). NASA implementation plan for education 1999-2003. Available:
http://education.nasa.gov/implan/role.html

[5] NASA. (no date). NASA field center education Web sites. Available:
http://education.nasa.gov/fldctr1.html

[6] Swissair (no date) Information about the accident of SR111. Available:
http://www.swissair.com/info111.htm

[7] News release reproduced from Swissair (1998, September) Information about the accident of SR111. Available:
http://www.swissair.com/press_releases/pressrel_030998_0930-en.htm

[8] See, for example, the Febreze thread in the alt.animals.felines newsgroup. Available through DejaNews at:

http://www.deja.com/[ST_rn=qs]/getdoc.xp?AN=464875941&
CONTEXT=924191789.183697536&hitnum=60

[9] Procter & Gamble (1998). Febreze - Safely cleans away odors on fabrics. Available:
http://www.febreze.com/pet.html

Chapter 9. Caveats & Constraints

Ethics, Urban Legends, Spoofs, Hoaxes, & Myths

Learning Objectives

This chapter focuses on some of the practical and ethical challenges of public relations through CMC. Major topics covered in the next few pages include:

➢ Hoaxes, myths, and urban legends.
➢ Ethical issues.
➢ Legal issues.
➢ Limitations of CMC for public relations.

New Challenges for Public Relations

Up to this point, we've looked at ways in which
practitioners might use CMC for public relations
programs and campaigns. But new technologies bring
with them new challenges and constraints. This
chapter describes several of the most common
concerns the practitioner should keep in mind when
using the Internet for public relations.

Hoaxes, Spoofs, Myths, & Urban Legends

We saw in Chapter 8 that Procter & Gamble has used
the Web to combat a rumor about its product Febreze.
This rumor and others like it circulate the 'Net with
alarming regularity. Anyone using the Internet will
eventually receive a bogus e-mail message that
announces a "new" hoax, myth, or urban legend.
Some of these messages announce fake viruses;
others request a good deed for someone in trouble;
still others are simply scare stories.

Proliferation of Internet Hoaxes, Myths, & Legends

There are a number of reasons for the proliferation of
false messages on the Internet. Occasionally, they
seem to be instigated to target a particular
organization, such as the AOL4FREE hoax "virus" or
the "Neiman-Marcus $250 Cookie Recipe." Here, the

bogus virus or the urban legend is linked with an
organizational name, in an apparent attempt to harass
the organization. Other types of illegitimate messages
seem more in the category of pranksterism, such as
the urban legend that relates a tale of the person
awaking in a tub of ice with a message to call 911,
and discovering that a kidney has been removed. Still
others may once have had some legitimacy, but over
the years have taken on lives of their own. All of
them are circulated and recirculated by well-meaning
but naïve new users, who unthinkingly send them to
all their friends and acquaintances without first
checking them for validity and accuracy.

One of the most enduring Internet chain letters has
plagued the Make-A-Wish Foundation® for years.
Several versions exist, but most make a plea to send
nine-year-old cancer patient Craig Shergold a
greeting card or business card to make his wish of
receiving enough cards to qualify for the *Guinness
Book of World Records* a reality. This request was
valid in 1989, but by 1990, the boy had received 16
million cards, and his wish was fulfilled. In March
1991, Shergold's brain tumor was removed
successfully, but the letter, which was not distributed
by Make-A-Wish Foundation, continued to circulate
on the Internet. In spite of major print and television
coverage and repeated pleas from Make-A-Wish
Foundation, the letter periodically continues to
resurface. Make-A-Wish Foundation has been forced
to install a special 800 telephone number to explain
the situation, and a section of its Web site is devoted
to it.[1]

How to Recognize a Hoax, Myth, or Urban Legend

Fake warnings of viruses and Trojan horses often sound very technical, and often seem to come from apparently valid sources, such as e-mail addresses of respected organizations or trusted friends. However, your friend may simply have sent the message to you in a moment of gullibility, or the organizational e-mail address may not belong to a well-qualified individual. Often, a letter will circulate repeatedly with just a few variables altered, such as names. If you see such a message, *don't* forward it until you are sure of your facts. Think about it critically, like any other information you find on the Internet. Look especially for the following telltale signs of a hoax:

1. The language looks suspiciously familiar; you've seen it before in a false message.
2. There is no date of origination in the body of the message ("forwarded" dates don't count).
3. The body of the message does not include the originator's name, e-mail address, and organizational affiliation.
4. Technical language sounds impressive but has no real substance.
5. The sender does not provide specific information on where or how the message has been validated.

There are a number of excellent Web sites that track hoaxes, spoofs, myths, viruses, and urban legends on the Internet. Bookmark a few of your favorites, and use them regularly when you're faced with questionable information.

Practicing Ethical Public Relations on the Internet

Legal and ethical issues are not necessarily mutually exclusive on the Internet. Both continue to evolve, and both are the subjects of hot debate. However, this chapter offers a few guidelines for the practitioner.

New technologies are forcing practitioners and hobbyists alike to face new legal and ethical challenges. The following sections describe some ethical issues on the Internet, and offer recommendations for public relations practitioners. Naturally, if you are a member of PRSA or IABC or some other professional association that has a code of ethical conduct, that code should form the grounding of your ethical decisions on the Internet.

Spamming

Spamming was covered in Chapter 6, within the context of "netiquette." However, it also is an ethical issue, because it often is done from forged or invalid addresses so recipients of the spam cannot contact the originators. Clearly, this practice is unethical, and it can result in loss of your e-mail account if the originating address is traced.

If you want to send a widely cast message to a large Internet audience, make sure, as you would with any other public relations message, that the audience is receptive. Obviously, this means that the people you are targeting must be interested in the topic and willing to receive information from you. It also means that you need to know what sort of connectivity your potential recipients have before you inundate them with large amounts of email or documents. If they are using a company system, for example, the company may monitor and limit mailbox content and size. Other systems base their rates on e-mail volume. If your recipients are inconvenienced by your unsolicited e-mail, you stand to lose far more than you gain.

If you receive spam from an unidentifiable source, you can contact the ISP "postmaster" (often the address is something like `postmaster@domainname.com`). Sometimes, the ISP is able to trace the originator of the message, and most ISPs are intolerant of spamming or sending illegal and unsolicited advertisements through their servers.

Use of Images and Other Materials

This issue is both ethical and legal, but is included under ethics because the ethics of misappropriating material are even broader than the legal issues. The ease of copying graphics images and text from the Internet often tempts beginners to use them without permission. There are literally hundreds of Web sites that offer graphics free of charge, and still more that will create customized graphics for nominal fees. Some of the sites offer "linkware," which means the images can be used without charge, but a link back to the site (usually with a mandated image for the hotlink) is required. However, it's *always* ethical to include attribution for the work of others.

It is both unethical and illegal to use copyrighted images without permission or attribution. Furthermore, a number of organizations rigorously enforce and protect their copyrighted materials on the Internet. The Electronic Frontier Foundation points out that "if you use copyrighted material in your multimedia project without getting permission, the owner of the copyright can prevent the distribution of your product and obtain damages from you for infringement, even if you did not intentionally include his or her material."[2]

Self-Identification in Discussion Lists & Newsgroups

Monitoring and participating in e-mail discussion lists and Usenet newsgroups can be a useful tool for early identification of issues and communication with emerging target publics. However, the practice also has certain ethical implications. Consider, for example, the possibility of monitoring a software users' newsgroup. If you represent a software developer, most professional codes of ethics mandate that you disclose your relationship with the client if you post that the client's software can solve a particular problem. This is both ethical and advantageous, because many newsgroup members are likely to appreciate having an "expert" available when questions about the product or service arise.

Cookies, Registration, & Online Surveys

A great deal of information about visitors to your Web site can be gathered through the use of cookies, registrations to use the site, and online surveys. Any data gathered about people means there is an ethical concern about how those data are used. Web sites that are designed with ethics in mind explain how cookies are set, what they do, and how the information will be gathered. Similarly, survey participants should be given an opportunity to decline having their information shared with other organizations or mailing lists.

The Ten Commandments of Computer Ethics

When in doubt, it's helpful to have a set of guidelines. Computer Professionals for Social Responsibility (CPSR) has published "Ten Commandments of Computer Ethics on Its Web Site." The commandments are:

1. Thou shalt not use a computer to harm other people.
2. Thou shalt not interfere with other people's computer work.
3. Thou shalt not snoop around in other people's computer files.
4. Thou shalt not use a computer to steal.
5. Thou shalt not use a computer to bear false witness.

6. Thou shalt not copy or use proprietary software for which you have not paid.
7. Thou shalt not use other people's computer resources without authorization or proper compensation.
8. Thou shalt not appropriate other people's intellectual output.
9. Thou shalt think about the social consequences of the program you are writing or the system you are designing.
10. Thou shalt always use a computer in ways that insure consideration and respect for your fellow humans.[3]

Legal Issues: Privacy & Security

Privacy is probably more illusion than fact when it comes to using the Internet. Issues of privacy and security stem both from system configurations and from user error. All too often, users compromise their own security by sharing their passwords or misusing a system. The ease of using a "reply" button results in a message being broadcast to an entire list that is intended for only one member of that list. There are hundreds of horror stories. The *Los Angeles Times*, for example, reported that "One job-seeker mistakenly sent his resume and a letter to a 1,000-person mailing list rather than to the hiring manager, [inadvertently] divulging salary demands and why he wanted the job."[4] Clearly, this means the practitioner should be very careful when working with mailing lists and discussion groups on behalf of a client.

The second issue of privacy and security stems from access and system flaws. Hackers and system administrators often have the ability to intercept, read, and archive e-mail messages without the knowledge of either the sender or the recipient. Fortunately, they rarely are interested in doing so.

Although issues of privacy and security are important to everyone, they most concern the practitioner when company e-mail accounts are involved. The Electronic Communications Privacy Act (ECPA) of 1986 protects user accounts. It amends the federal wiretap law and makes accessing stored electronic messages by breaking into an electronic system or exceeding authorized access a criminal offense.[5] However, many organizations use electronic means to supervise employees and consider messages stored on company servers to be company property. Here, it is important to notify employees up front, both online and offline, about company policy as it pertains to transmission and storage of electronic messages.

Limitations of the Internet for Public Relations

Most of this text has focused on the advantages and disadvantages of using the Internet for public relations. However, CMC is not a panacea for improved communications between a client and its publics. Not all publics can be reached through computers, so other means of communication should work with your online efforts. It's easy to fall into the trap of assuming everyone has computers when you're surrounded by them, but many pockets of the U.S. population and even more people abroad have limited or no access to computers. In addition, some segments of the population may have access, but have minimal computer expertise. These people often are reluctant to communicate through e-mail, chat rooms, or other forms of CMC.

As mentioned in Chapter 6, it's important to remember that ISPs, personal computers, and individual configurations vary widely. Home users often do not upgrade equipment as frequently as businesses. Thus, they may not have the state-of-the-art hardware and software your high-end multimedia Web site requires. For these target publics, consider designing the site for lower-end computers or integrating alternative ways to view the site that require less bandwidth.

If you're targeting a professional clientele, you probably can assume a faster connection than if you're targeting the home user. Typically, though, not-for-profit organizations, which rely on donated goods and services, will not have state-of-the-art hardware and software. The bottom line, here, is to design your online communications just as you would your offline communications—with the target public's attitudes, values, and lifestyles in mind.

Chapter Summary

This chapter addressed issues of ethics and legality that affect public relations on the Internet. Ethical online public relations avoids spamming, does not misappropriate images or text, provides appropriate attribution, discloses client ties in public communications, and notifies users of policies concerning privacy and security. Limitations of the

Internet for public relations include limited or no
access, minimal user expertise, and user capability
hardware and software insufficiencies.

Exercises

1. Visit several graphics archives on the Web (use a keyword search for "free graphics"). Review the policies for linkware, freeware, and work for hire. If you designed graphics, what type of policy do you think you would develop for distributing your work?

2. Visit several of your favorite online shopping sites. What are their policies concerning your privacy? Are they clearly stated?

3. Think about your company or school. Does it have a policy concerning Internet communication? Is it easily accessible for all employees or students?

References

Brinson, J. D., & Radcliffe, M. F. (1996). *An intellectual property law primer for multimedia and Web developers.* Electronic Frontier Foundation. Available:
http://www.eff.org/pub/CAF/law/ip-primer

Computer Ethics Institute. (1997). *The ten commandments of computer ethics.* Computer Professionals for Social Responsibility (CPSR). Available:
http://www.cpsr.org/program/ethics/cei.html

Hernandez, R. T. (1987). *Computer electronic mail and privacy.* Paper written at California Western School of Law.

Kapor, M. (1992). Computer spies. *Forbes*, 150(11): 288.

Keubelbeck, A. (1991). Getting the message. *Los Angeles Times*, 110, E1-2 (September 4)

Make-A-Wish Foundation® of America. (no date). *Chain Letters (Craig Shergold & Ryan McGhee).* Available:
http://www.wish.org/craig.htm

PRSA. (no date). *PRSA's Code of Professional Standards.* Available:
http://www.prsa.org/profstd.html

U.S. Department of Energy (1999). Computer Incident Advisory Capability. *CIAC Internet Hoaxes.* Available:
http://www.ciac.org/ciac/CIACHoaxes.html

Notes

[1] Make-A-Wish Foundation® of America. (no date). *Chain Letters (Craig Shergold & Ryan McGhee).* Available: http://www.wish.org/craig.htm

[2] Brinson, J. D., & Radcliffe, M. F. (1996). *An intellectual property law primer for multimedia and Web developers.* Electronic Frontier Foundation. Available: http://www.eff.org/pub/CAF/law/ip-primer

[3] Computer Ethics Institute. (1997). *The ten commandments of computer ethics.* Computer Professionals for Social Responsibility (CPSR). Available: http://www.cpsr.org/program/ethics/cei.html

[4] Keubelbeck, A. (1991). Getting the message. *Los Angeles Times*, 110, E1-2 (September 4).

[5] Hernandez, R. T. (1987). *Computer electronic mail and privacy.* Paper written at California Western School of Law.

Appendix A. Beginning HTML Tags

Note: XXXX represents variable information (such as background color, file name, etc.). **Be sure to use quotation marks and other symbols exactly as shown. File names must be short with appropriate extensions, and must match *exactly* the way they appear in the html code.**

TAG	WHAT IT MEANS
<HTML></HTML>	Beginning & end of html document
<BODY background="./filename.gif"></BODY>	Body text with relative link to background graphic
<BODY BGCOLOR="#XXXXXX" TEXT="#XXXXXX" LINK="#XXXXXX">	Specification of background, text, and link colors.
<TITLE></TITLE>	Title of document (appears in top bar)
<CENTER></CENTER>	Center Text
<H1></H1>	First Header
<H2></H2>	Second Header
<H3></H3>	Third Header
<P>	Paragraph break (skips one line space)
 	Move down one line space (like a carriage return)
<IMG SRC="./filename.gif">	Inserts an inline image (relative path link)
<IMG SRC="http://domain/filename.gif">	Inserts an inline image (fixed path link)
<IMG SRC="./filename.gif" ALT="text">	Display text for browsers that can't read images
<A HREF="./filename.html">your text</A>	Hotlink to another document (relative path)
<A HREF="http://domain/filename.html">your text</A>	Hotlink to another document (fixed path)

`<UL>`
  `<LI> red`
  `<LI> blue`
  `<LI> yellow`
`</UL>`
	Unnumbered bulleted list:
	• red
	• blue
	• yellow

`<OL>`
  `<LI> strawberry`
  `<LI> blueberry`
  `<LI> lemon`
`</OL>`
	Numbered list:
	1. strawberry
	2. blueberry
	3. lemon

`<DL>`
  `<DT> Strawberry`
    `<DD> A sweet fruit rich in vitamin`
C.
  `<DT> Blueberry`
    `<DD> A small, deep blue berry.`
  `</DL>`
	Definition list::
	Strawberry
	  A sweet fruit rich in vitamin C.
	Blueberry
	  A small, deep blue berry.

`<PRE></PRE>`	Preformatted text.
`<HR>`	Horizontal Rule
`<B>`	Bold Text
`<I>`	Italic Text
`<TT>`	Typewriter text (e.g., fixed width font)
`<A HREF="mailto:loginid@host">` `Name</A>`	Hotlink for a "mailto" pop-up box
`<TABLE></TABLE>`	Begins and ends a table
`<CAPTION></CAPTION>`	Defines a caption for table title
`<TH></TH>`	Defines table header (default is bold, centered)
`<TR></TR>`	Specifies a row within a table
`<TD></TD>`	Specifies a table data cell

File Type	Extension
Plain text	.txt
HTML document	.html
GIF image	.gif
Secure HTML document	.shtml
TIFF image	.tiff
X Bitmap image	.xbm
JPEG image	.jpg or .jpeg
PostScript file	.ps
AIFF sound file	.aiff
AU sound file	.au
WAV sound file (IBM)	.wav
QuickTime movie	.mov
MPEG movie	.mpeg or .mpg

Glossary

Terms & Acronyms

A

Adaptive structuration theory
A model based on Giddens' structuration metatheory that encompasses the relationships between social groups and technology.

Analog
An infinite array of continuous values.

Annotated directory
Web site that provides lists of hotlinks to selected Web sites, along with a brief summary of each.

Archie
A search engine for the Internet that locates primarily FTP archives.

ARPANet
Predecessor of the Internet.

ASCII
American Standard Code for Information Exchange. This is a universally used computer code for letters and characters.

Asynchronous communication

Also known as nonsimultaneous communication.
Communication during which participants engage in
the process at different times, such as bulletin boards
or e-mail.

B

Bandwidth

The channels of communication that are available in
CMC, which often is considered to have "narrow
bandwidth," because of its lack of face-to-face
nonverbal cues.

Baud

(BPS) The speed of data transmission, as measured
by number of bits per second.

Bit

Binary Digit. The smallest measure of data
transmission as a single pulse of electricity,
mathematically represented as a "0" or "1."

Bitmap

A data file that corresponds bit for bit with the image
displayed on a screen. Characterized by the
measurement in pixels. The number of bits per pixel
determines the number of shades of grays or colors
the image displays.

BITNET

Named after an IBM ad that read, "Because It's
Time," a network of computer systems that is

separate from the Internet, although it can receive and transmit mail through the Internet.

Boolean search

Among the oldest and most widely used of search techniques, based on logical mathematical operators. Connects words together in particular ways, such as "and," "or," and "not."

BPS

(Baud) The speed of data transmission, as measured by number of bits per second.

Byte

A measure of data transmission equal to eight bits, and typically the equivalent of one typed keyboard character.

C

Cathode Ray Tube

The monitor or display for a television or computer. CRTs display images by exciting phosphor dots with a scanned electron beam (the "ray").

Central processing unit

(CPU) The portion of the computer that performs calculations that allow it to operate. Also sometimes called the central processor or processor.

Central processor

The portion of the computer that performs calculations that allow it to operate. Also sometimes called the central processing unit (CPU) or processor.

CMC

(Computer-mediated communication) Any form of interpersonal, small group, organizational, or public communication that occurs with the use of computers.

Computer Codes

Sets of characters that instruct computer systems to perform certain functions.

Computer-mediated communication

(CMC) Any form of interpersonal, small group, organizational, or public communication that occurs with the use of computers.

Cost per person

(CPM) How much it costs to reach each member of a targeted audience.

CPU

(Central processing unit) The portion of the computer that performs calculations that allow it to operate. Also sometimes called the central processor or processor.

CREN

Corporation for Research and Educational Networking.

CRT

(Cathode Ray Tube) The monitor or display for a television or computer. CRTs display images by exciting phosphor dots with a scanned electron beam (the "ray").

D

Digital
Discrete and finite values.

Domain name
A name assigned to one or more IP addresses. Large companies, such as Microsoft, may have a dozen or more servers that share a single domain name. In the case of Microsoft, the domain name is microsoft.com

Download
Transfer a file or document from a host computer to a personal computer.

DPI
Dots Per Inch. In printing parlance, dpi refers to the number of dots per inch in a halftone. Web images are usually low resolution—about 72 dpi, which means there are 72 *pixels* per inch in an image on the Web.

E

Emoticons
Also known as graphic accents. Pictures that are formed as groups of ASCII characters, for example, a "smiley face," which is created with a colon for eyes, a hyphen for a nose, and a parenthesis for a mouth.

:-)

Ethernet
A protocol that allows communication over local area networks.

F

FAQ

Frequently Asked Questions. A file that orients the
reader to a newsgroup, Web site, or other Internet
system by listing and answering commonly asked
questions.

Field searching

Limits searches to specific areas of a Web page, such
as the URL, the title, the headers, the links, the text,
or the images.

FidoNet

A worldwide network that enables exchanges e-mail,
discussion groups, and files through personal
computers. Originally for hobbyists and IBM-based,
FidoNet now accommodates PC, Mac, Unix, and
other systems.

Finger

A software program that allows a user to read another
user's public login information, which typically
consists of their name, login ID, and whether the
person is online at the moment. Some individuals
append additional information files to their login
directories.

Flaming

Uninhibited remarks that are generally considered
hostile. May include swearing, insults, or other
negative speech acts.

Freeware

Software that consumers can install and use on their computers free of charge.

FTP

(File Transfer Protocol) Allows computers to transfer files (documents, applications, graphics, etc.) across platforms. Many "anonymous ftp" libraries exist throughout the world, where users can log in as "anonymous" and transfer freeware and shareware.

G

Gatekeeper

A filter between source/receivers in the mechanistic model of communication.

Gateway

The server through which information travels between two computer systems or networks.

GDSS

(Group Decision Support System) A computer-based system that supports message exchange, collaboration on ideas, projects, and products, and/or group decision-making.

GIF

(Graphics Interchange Format) File format that enables users to transmit and receive high-quality graphic images. Developed by Compuserve Information Systems.

Gigabyte

One million bytes of information.

Gopher

A hierarchical, menu-based search and retrieval system on the Internet, originally developed at the University of Minnesota, and named after the University mascot.

Graphic accents

Also known as emoticons. Pictures created exclusively with ASCII characters, such as a "smiley face," which is created with a colon for eyes, a hyphen for a nose, and a parenthesis for a mouth.

:-)

Group Decision Support System

(GDSS) A computer-based system that supports message exchange, collaboration on ideas, projects, and products, and/or group decision-making.

H

html

(HyperText Markup Language) A computer code that creates hypertext documents for the World Wide Web.

http

(HyperText Transfer Protocol) Transfers hypertext documents across servers on the World Wide Web.

1135 Cedar Shoals Dr.
Athens, Georgia 30605

(706) 353-2632
Fax (706) 546-8417

Invitations
to media
"come and cover"

reformat
feature
pitches

How are
we doing

Hytelnet

An Internet-based browsing system of sites available via Telnet.

Hypertext

Computer interface that allows multiple types of messages (graphics, sound, etc.), as well as direct movement to documents across various servers on the World Wide Web. First coined by Theodor Nelson as a way to describe what he called "non-sequential writing."

HyperText Markup Language

(html) A computer code that creates hypertext documents for the World Wide Web.

HyperText Transfer Protocol

(http) Protocol that transfers hypertext documents across servers on the World Wide Web.

I, J, K

Infobot

Computer program that automatically sends information via the Internet to individuals who send queries to the server. Widely used for marketing and PR.

Internet

An amorphous, global, non-hierarchical network of computer networks, originally developed for scientific and military communication.

Internet Relay Chat

(IRC) Allows users to communicate interactively in real time (synchronously) with one or many other users via the Internet.

IP address

A unique Internet address that is designated by four sets of numbers separated by periods. Because numbers are difficult for most people to remember, IP addresses usually are assigned a domain name.

IRC

(Internet Relay Chat) Allows users to communicate interactively in real time (synchronously) with one or many other users via the Internet.

JPEG

(Joint Photographic Experts Group—also JPG) The name of the group that developed the compression algorithm by the same name for full color and grayscale image files.

JPG

See JPEG.

KWIC

(Keyword In Context). A search function that enables definition of the context in which the search terms appear by specifying words that should appear near the search terms.

L

Listproc
A distribution management software package for Internet-based subscription lists.

Listserv
A distribution management software package for Internet-based subscription lists.

Lycos
A Web-based search engine that is based at Carnegie Mellon.

M

Majordomo
A distribution management software package for Internet-based subscription lists.

Media Richness
The degree to which a medium facilitates feedback or provides multiple cues to reduce message ambiguity. Rich media are considered most efficient for highly ambiguous communication.

Mediated Communication
Communication that is mediated by a gatekeeper, usually used in reference to mass communication.

MIME
(Multipurpose Internet Mail Extension) Encapsulates non-ASCII documents for transmission via e-mail.

Both sender and receiver must have software to
handle MIME-encapsulated documents.

N

Netiquette
Etiquette on the Internet, often established by group
norms and/or official guidelines.

NNTP
(Network News Transfer Protocol) Allows users to
navigate Usenet newsgroups.

Nonsimultaneous communication
Also known as asynchronous communication.
Communication during which participants engage in
the process at different times, such as bulletin boards
or e-mail.

NREN
National Research and Education Network Program.

O

Operating System
(OS) The software that manages files and
applications, input of data from the keyboard, mouse
or touch screen, and output to printer, monitor and
other peripheral devices.

P

PEM

Privacy Enhanced Mail.

PGP

Pretty Good Privacy. An encryption program for e-mail.

Ping

A program that traces the route between two sites and the time required for data to be transmitted between them.

Pixel

Derived from the term, **Pic**ture **El**ement, a pixel is the smallest point of a graphic image. The more pixels per inch, the higher the resolution. Web images are usually low resolution—about 72 *dpi* (dots per inch), which means there are 72 pixels per inch in an image on the Web.

POP

Post Office Protocol. The protocol through which e-mail is downloaded from the computer server to the user.

Processor

The portion of the computer that performs calculations that allow it to operate. Also sometimes called the central processing unit (CPU) or central processor.

Protocol

A specialized combination of hardware and software that enables computers with different operating systems to communicate.

Q, R

Random Access Memory

(RAM) Computer memory that can be accessed randomly, and which is erased when the power is shut off.

S

Server

Any computer or other device that manages network resources.

Shareware

Software that consumers can install and use on their computers for nominal fees to help pay for development. Usually, shareware can be used at no charge for a short period on a trial basis.

SIG

Special Interest Group. Can be synchronous (e.g., IRC or chat room) or asynchronous (e.g., e-mail).

Simultaneous communication

Also known as synchronous communication. Communication during which participants engage in the process at the same time, such as a telephone conversation or Internet chat room.

SMTP
(Simple Mail Transfer Protocol) A *protocol* that processes electronic mail.

Snail Mail
Traditional land/air mail, so called because of its relative slowness, in comparison to e-mail.

Spamming
Sending unsolicited mass e-mail to members of e-mail discussion lists or Usenet newsgroups.

Structuration
Frames social structures as being formed through human interactions.

Synchronous communication
Also known as simultaneous communication. Communication during which participants engage in the process at the same time, such as a telephone conversation or Internet chat room.

Sysop
System operator or administrator. The individual responsible for running a computer system, BBS, etc.

Systems Theory
A view of the communicative process as a system.

Systems
Entities that function as a result of the interdependent action of its components (subsystems). A closed system is neither sensitive to its environment, nor does it make adjustments for external events (e.g., a wristwatch). An open system is sensitive to

environmental influences, and may have internal mechanisms for adjustment (e.g., an organization).

T

TCP/IP

(Transmission Control Protocol/Internet Protocol) The primary transport protocols of the Internet.

Telnet

A protocol that allows computers with different operating systems to communicate over the Internet, it is available as applications for both IBM-compatible and Macintosh computers. Once the Telnet application is launched and a connection with a host computer is made, all transactions within the Telnet window are conducted on the local computer in terminal emulation.

Terminal Emulation

Commands a computer to behave like a host computer to which it is connected. Terminal emulation programs allow connections to bulletin boards and mainframe computers from personal computers.

Truncation search

Supports the use of a "wild card" symbol to search for various forms of a particular word.

U

Uniform Resource Locator

(URL) The global address of Web pages and other Web resources; the Web page equivalent of an e-mail address.

Unix

A multi-user operating system that was originally developed by Bell Labs. Although Unix is not user friendly, it is a powerful OS that can be accessed from remote computers, and it allows users to perform a variety of online tasks.

Upload

Transfer a file or document from a personal computer to a host computer.

URL

(Uniform Resource Locator) The global address of Web pages and other Web resources; the Web page equivalent of an e-mail address.

Usenet

A distributed bulletin board system that is accessible through the Internet. Usenet consists largely of Unix servers and offers users more than 25,000 discussion groups.

UUCP

Unix-to-Unix Copy Program.

V

Validity

The accuracy of information. In the natural and social sciences, issues of validity concern whether a study measures what it claims to measure.

VERONICA

Very Easy Rodent-Oriented Net-wide Index to Computerized Archives. This is an Internet-based search engine for Gopher.

VRML

Virtual Reality Markup Language. Coding to create three-dimensional graphics on the Web.

W

WAIS

Wide Area Information Server. Databases typically of text-based documents that are available via the Internet.

Whois

Internet white page search engine for finding e-mail addresses of individuals or organizations.

WWW

World Wide Web. A network of servers that are dedicated to hypertext document storage and retrieval.

X, Y, Z

Yahoo

A Web-based search engine that was originally developed at Stanford.

Index

Names & Terms